If Brené Brown were to write to a religious audience, I imagine this book would be it. Part memoir, part sermon, Kurt Francom, host of the groundbreaking *Leading Saints* podcast, will disrupt your view of God. It's a balm in Gilead for anyone who wants to know they matter, really matter, to Him. Inspiring, riveting, powerful.

—Whitney Johnson, CEO of Disruption Advisors, a Thinkers50 Top 10 Management Thinker, and *Wall Street Journal* Best-Selling Author

I believe the core message of this book is one of the most-needed and most-overlooked messages of our time. As he always does, Kurt Francom brings his incredible wisdom, experience, and candidness to a topic that has the potential to bless the lives of many. I will be giving this book away to all my loved ones. A must-read for people of faith.

—Jody Moore, Life Coach

If you feel drawn to *Is God Disappointed in Me?* it's probably because 1) you fear the answer is yes; 2) you hope the answer is no; and 3) you still worry that without disappointment and fear you won't be motivated to change and you'll never be "enough." Take heart! The motivation for heart-level change is not based on either God's disappointment or our own but on learning to let His love, mercy, and healing in more deeply. I love this inspiring, practical, and compassionate book!

—Wendy Ulrich, PhD, Psychologist, and Author

I recently worked with someone suffering from shame. He was struggling with whether he was a good person or a bad person when the real issue was that he was someone who needed to be healed. Our doctrine does not imagine a puritan God, but sometimes that is the image we conjure of Him.

Nothing is worse than feeling we may be disappointing God, especially when such an idea is so wrongheaded.

This book is a powerful and insightful exploration of the impact of shame and disappointment on our relationship with God and ourselves. Francom's personal experiences and struggles with shame and disappointment are relatable and will resonate universally. This book offers a practical framework for avoiding unnecessary feelings of disappointment and fostering a deeper, more meaningful relationship with God, providing a valuable resource for anyone seeking to overcome shame and disappointment and connect with their true identity in Christ.

—Greg McKeown, Author of *New York Times* Best Sellers *Effortless* and *Essentialism*, Podcaster

This is a valuable book that will push readers to more carefully examine some of their key assumptions. Kurt's writing is filled with warmth and compassion—I'm already looking forward to rereading this book!

—John Hilton III, Author of *Considering the Cross* and the Seeking Jesus Course

A tremendous read! Kurt Francom's insight on the true nature of God and His love for us is a fresh breath of hope and peace in a world where it is so desperately needed. *Is God Disappointed in*

Me? offers a unique approach to the power of grace and how God's acceptance and love can propel us into a relationship with Him through covenants and commandments that lift and bless.

—Clint Pulver, Emmy Award Winner, Keynote Speaker, and Best-Selling Author of *I Love It Here*

If there is one thing the world needs more of, it is love and hope. The ultimate source of this grace is found in a relationship with God. Oftentimes, we talk about the "what in the Gospel" but don't understand the "how." In *Is God Disappointed in Me?* Kurt addresses the how with vulnerable examples and divine accessibility. We need more shame-busting books to guide us along the path of discipleship. This is one of those books.

—Ganel-Lyn Condie, Speaker, *Talk of Him* Podcast Host, Best-Selling Author

A beautiful exploration of God's character and our relationship with Him, Kurt Francom's book hits the sweet spot between carefully crafted new insight and rubber-hits-the-road, real-life experience. Bring your highlighter because there are thoughtful gems throughout which you'll want to mark and refer to again and again.

—Carrie L. Skarda, Psychologist

The opening pages of this book may resonate with you like they did with me, with Kurt recounting the youthful fear of talking to the bishop to such an empathetic degree that you will be unable to stop reading until you learn of Kurt's powerful suggestions for working through the thoughts everyone has in striving to live the gospel. *Is God Disappointed in Me?* may be one of the most important books our youth can read, not to mention leaders, parents, and those interested in teaching more carefully about the enemy's grasp of shame, our divine worth and identity, and coming to grips with embracing the Atonement in our lives. This is a MUST READ for anyone looking to come closer to our Savior and God, who is our Father first and foremost! He knows the end score; we live and watch the game differently when we know who wins: we ALL win!

—Jason Hewlett, CSP, CPAE, Author of
The Promise to the One, Hall of Fame Speaker,
Award-Winning Entertainer

My only regret after having read *Is God Disappointed in Me?* for the first time is that I didn't take notes. Kurt Francom's down-to-earth, practical, yet profound wisdom is needed today more than ever before. Every chapter explores a principle that resonates to the core as true, timeless, familiar, and yet somehow elusive. This book examines ideals that you know are true but that sometimes you still need to be *told* are true. Francom understands the challenges Latter-day Saints face today on an incredibly relatable level. Every teenager needs to read it. Every parent needs to read it. Everyone needs to read it.

—David Snell, Host of *Saints Unscripted*

IS GOD DISAPPOINTED IN ME?

IS GOD DISAPPOINTED IN ME?

Removing Shame from a Gospel of Grace

KURT FRANCOM

**Foreword by Brad Pelo,
President & Executive Producer of *The Chosen***

Copyright © 2023 by Kurt Francom

All rights reserved, including the right to reproduce this book, or portions thereof, in any form. No part of this book may be used or reproduced in any manner whatsoever without written permission from the publisher, except in the case of brief quotations embodied in critical articles and reviews. For information or permission, contact the author at LeadingSaints.org/contact.

This is a work of creative nonfiction. The events herein are portrayed to the best of the author's memory. While all the stories in this book are true, some names and identifying details may have been changed to protect the privacy of the people involved.

Cover design by MiblArt
Print design and layout by Michelle Nelson
Ebook design and layout by Sydnee Hyer

Published by Leading Saints

979-8-9882472-0-3 paperback
979-8-9882472-1-0 eBook

To my children. Know this one thing:
God was never disappointed in you.

Contents

Foreword	xiii
Introduction	1
1 The Projected False God	9
2 Godly Disappointment	15
3 Behaviors versus Heart	37
4 Identity	59
5 Hold On to Commandments	81
6 Vulnerable Wounds	93
7 Hide, Numb, or Heal	111
8 The Raging Love of God	135
9 Grace for Grace	149
10 Leading with Love	163
11 Conclusion	177
Acknowledgments	181
Notes	183
Note to the Reader	189
About the Author	191

Foreword

In 2022, I accompanied Dallas Jenkins, creator of the TV series The Chosen, to an event at Utah State University. He was invited to participate as part of the Leonard J. Arrington Mormon History Lecture Series. Dallas, an Evangelical, was an unlikely guest. While he enjoyed a devoted following in the Bible Belt, Northern Utah seemed an unlikely venue for the son of Jerry Jenkins, a celebrated author of Evangelical books.

As it turns out, Dallas was not only welcome, but many students had to be turned away after the auditorium was filled to capacity. During the Q&A portion of the evening, students asked Dallas about his relationship with Latter-day Saints and whether or not he had plans to make a sequel to *The Chosen* based on The Book of Mormon account of Jesus's visit to the Americas. (His answer was an emphatic no.)

The most memorable parts of our visit that night were the conversations that occurred after his speech, when audience members lined up to meet Dallas. My proximity to him allowed me to overhear dozens of conversations, many tear-filled and sincere. I overheard a chorus of thank-yous, but many expressions also included something else. "Thank you for depicting a Jesus that might actually love me . . . forgive me . . . be my friend." "Thank you for depicting Jesus in full color rather than the black-and-white version that I grew up with." I heard the same thing, although with variation, dozens of times throughout the night.

People had been deeply moved, not only by the story of *The Chosen* but by a depiction of Jesus as a personage of love who champions God's children while defending them from hypocrites. He laughs and dances and comforts people during their relapses and struggles. Through Dallas's work people are encountering a portrayal of a Jesus who is relational rather than transactional.

It was late that night when we finally left campus, hungrier than expected. Thirty minutes later, we were sharing a family-sized platter of wings while Dallas questioned me in the privacy of an empty restaurant. He wondered why Latter-day Saints, which we both assumed made up the majority of attendees that night, had such a profound experience with his depiction of Jesus in *The Chosen*. I shared some of my own life experiences as a Latter-day Saint, a missionary, twice a bishop, a member of a YSA stake presidency, and a father of twelve children.

I had spent countless hours with fellow Latter-day Saint neighbors, friends, and children who struggled to believe that Jesus, let alone a "loving" Father, wanted anything to do with them in their broken state. I had felt those feelings of shame and rejection myself. I had hung my head as a teen while talking to my bishop about sinful behavior and had repeated that shame-rooted confession many times before I came to know for myself that our Savior is not repelled by us but lovingly pursues us, not in spite of our sins but, in part, because of them. He's not horrified by our wounds, whether self-inflicted or otherwise.

IS GOD DISAPPOINTED IN ME?

In the pages of this book, Kurt Francom introduces you to a Savior and Father who are both "in our corner," a phrase mentioned in the book and taken from the boxing world.

After each round in a boxing match, the contender returns to his corner of the ring, where a trainer and medic set out a stool for him to sit and rest. No matter how beaten and bloodied he might be, his two supporters are there to treat his wounds while offering perspective, correction, and encouragement. Bandaged and renewed, he returns to the ring.

Our Father and Savior aren't in the arena cheering for us one moment and booing the next. They don't walk out when we're knocked down or even knocked out. They stand in our corner, remaining close without interfering, ready to offer aid. At times we drown out Their voices during the fight, but it doesn't mean They aren't there, and, no, They're not passively observing, just waiting for us to shamefully present ourselves in defeat.

When we turn to find refuge in the corner, whether running or crawling, They reach out; lift us; wipe our blood, sweat, and tears; rub our shoulders; and whisper in our ear. Their voices still us and bring our heart rate down, for they are voices of love, of invitation, of conviction, and of courage, for They have already won the fight for us. Our victory is sure even if we doubt that truth.

As you read this book, I invite you to open yourself up to a God who is not only *not* disappointed in you but Who actually delights in you. He is *not* standing in continuous judgment but rather in persistent, never-ending love. President Ezra Taft Benson said, "Nothing will surprise us more than when we get to heaven and see the Father and realize how well we know Him and how familiar His face is to us"[1]—not only His face but His adoring gaze. He is not

xv

ashamed of us. We are His children. And though our own mortal parents may not have modeled that type of love, He's offering it to us still. He was the perfect parent in heaven, and He is the perfect parent now.

Our Father bestowed us with an identity frequently obscured by the noise of the world, counterfeit voices in our heads, and the shame of our choices. We can return to true identity, restored relationships, and hope in our journey, and we can do so now. Whether you're in the depths of addiction, experiencing loss, or have given up hope for another reason, the message and perspective on these pages will aid you in experiencing true identity again and the relationship the Father and His Son are anxious to restore.

—Brad Pelo, President and Executive Producer,
The Chosen

Introduction

Back in 1998, as a sixteen-year-old, I was sure God was disappointed in me. I remember sitting in our family room while my mom folded laundry and watched a slow-paced crime drama on TV. I was looking at the TV, but my focus went directly through the screen as if it wasn't there. My mind was elsewhere, battling with the reality and shame of some regrettable actions I had made in the previous few months. I no longer felt like the timid, good boy I used to be. I had found a way to take steps toward a dangerous edge of sin, and nobody but I knew what I had done. Shame, guilt, and personal disappointment filled my soul, and I knew I had gone too far just to shrug it off and dismiss it. I was desperate for help and guidance, and I didn't know what to do. In reality, I did know what to do, but the steps of reaching out to someone, including my bishop, seemed scary and impossible because so many people would be disappointed in me. I thought God would be disappointed in me as well.

In that moment of despair, I opened my mouth and said, "Mom, I think there is something wrong with me." I remember my mom returned my statement with a short line of encouragement and then got back to her task at hand. I don't blame her for not saying more, as it was a strange time to reach out for help. But I didn't know what else to do.

Feeling like my cry for help had failed, I figured I would go directly to my bishop. He was my former youth leader before his call, so I knew him relatively well and trusted him. However, knowing him so well made me assume that I'd be met with more disappointment. A few days later, I decided to make the call. I went into my parents' bedroom and closed the door for some privacy, as my parents still had no idea about the spiritual struggle I was experiencing. I sat down and grabbed the phone on the nightstand. Before I could dial the executive secretary's phone number to make an appointment, the shame of my situation buried me again. I was sure that calling this nice, older man who handled the bishop's schedule meant I would have to recount all my slipups to him, leading to one more person being disappointed in me. Somehow, I still made the call and was relieved when it was shorter than I expected. The call felt more like setting a dentist appointment than an execution date.

Before I knew it, my appointment had arrived on a clear Sunday afternoon. I made a lousy excuse to my parents, saying I was headed to the church to help my quorum with an assignment. I still couldn't bring myself to open up to them because I was sure they would be disappointed that their son had to confess something to the bishop. I arrived at the church and found a seat just far enough away from the bishop's office so nobody would see me, but close enough so the bishop knew I was there.

I hated this! Why did I get myself in this situation? Each step of this process further convinced me that I was the only youth in my ward's history to ever set an appointment with the bishop to confess something. Maybe this meeting was a mistake; perhaps I could figure this out on my own. I knew the bishop had been proud of me

IS GOD DISAPPOINTED IN ME?

as a former youth leader, and now I was going to shatter his perception of me. I wanted the building to collapse on me or to run away and act like none of this ever happened. Sitting outside the bishop's office convinced me that I was broken, that I was beyond repair, and worst of all, that I had disappointed my Father in Heaven.

At the time, I felt like it was a unique experience, but I discovered many years later, when I was a bishop, that this experience, especially for youth, is quite common. As a youth, I was an upstanding young man who had fulfilled most expectations of being a young Latter-day Saint. I had received all the priesthood ordinations related to the office of deacon, teacher, and priest, consistently blessed and passed the sacrament on Sundays, earned an Eagle Scout Award, and served in youth leadership. It was common to hear praise about me and the young man I was becoming. I also knew the doctrine as well as any other of my religious peers. I had hours of gospel instruction about repentance spanning back to my first nursery class, and many home evening lessons before that. I understood the doctrine of repentance and the glorious opportunity that the Atonement of Jesus Christ offered. But when I was about to exercise that gift for myself and rely personally on the Atonement, I felt unsalvageable.

This task buried me with shame, and I deeply feared the disappointment of others. On paper, I could explain the algebra of forgiveness and rattle off the five steps of repentance. I could rehearse statements about the miracle of Jesus Christ and the infinite powers of His Atonement. But they were just words now.

My journey to the bishop's office as a teenager ended well. My bishop was extraordinarily welcoming and loving, and we had several appointments in the weeks that followed. I never felt disappointment from him, and he helped me remove any shame I was feeling and turn toward Christ. Years later, as a bishop myself, I ran into this man. I hugged him with purpose, as I now understood how he helped me as a young man—I was now, as bishop of my own ward, striving to be that comforting voice for others.

In short, this book is about the attacks we experience from the adversary through his strongest tool—shame. The word "disappointed" is on the cover and is discussed at length in this book. Disappointment is the feeling that sparks shame. Once that spark ignites, the adversary fuels it with more shame. This is the strongest tool of the adversary because it is a direct attack on identity. Shame makes us question who we are and whether we are broken beyond repair. If we are convinced that our identity is flawed and broken, we begin to feel disappointment and assume God feels the same way about us.

Disappointment is simply the transfer of shame within the boundaries of a loving relationship. We assume there was an expectation set, we missed it, and now we are not what God hoped we were.

This battle of shame and disappointment happens every day, everywhere, like with the mother who dedicates her life to raising her children but often gets trapped in the cycle of comparison through her social media feed. Scrolling through, she stops on a photo of a family sending off a clean-cut missionary or posing in front of a temple after a sealing ordinance. Other images show homes that are spotless and yards that are perfectly manicured. *They must have it all figured out, unlike me,* she thinks. This experience introduces feelings of disappointment in herself, which lead to feelings that God must have expected more of her as well. You see, she assumes this perception of a long list of expectations is what God is demanding. *Be a good mother and create a home that*

IS GOD DISAPPOINTED IN ME?

will foster love and testimony. Then she snaps at her five-year-old and, while being overcome by the sound of his crying, she realizes she still hasn't started dinner and there isn't a chance her *Come, Follow Me* lesson is going to happen at this point. With a toddler on her hip and another child wailing, she isn't just disappointed with herself but feels that God expects more out of her and she has failed.

What about the aging father getting close to being an empty nester? He and his wife had always talked about living in this "starter home" for only a few years. They had plans to build the ideal home to raise their family, like so many of their friends have done. Now their family is almost raised, and they are still there. His career has been mediocre compared to the dreams he once had, and his spiritual journey has been disappointing. He witnessed several of his friends and colleagues move through Church leadership ranks, serving in bishoprics and stake presidencies. His service experience only entailed watching nursery kids and twelve-year-old goof-offs. He never desired the busy Church leadership callings but figured that God must not trust him, since God always chose someone else instead of him. Maybe he doesn't have what it takes to lead on that level, he thinks. Once again, disappointment drives the shame deeper and deeper.

The adversary is determined to get us to turn away from God and reach for sin; however, sin is the goal for Satan, not the method. He cannot convince a Saint to turn to sin simply by suggesting sinful behavior. He must lay a foundation of corruption on the heart of man. For our hearts to be corrupted, we must let shame in. Shame, the most powerful tool of the adversary, is what causes us to question our identity.

Once we embrace this false identity, we turn to sin to numb the hurt. This is where disappointment becomes a powerful tool for the adversary. Disappointment facilitates the transfer of shame from one being to another. Disappointment is one of the strongest emotions in the human experience because it leaves us vulnerable to shame. Disappointment dominates thoughts and emotions like vinegar dominates taste. We can try to combat it with doctrinal reminders—*God loves all His children,* or *the Atonement is infinite*—like we can try mixing more milk with vinegar. When we take an ideal and mix it with disappointment, it only strengthens the disappointment and diminishes the ideal. Satan knows this, and when we, in a vulnerable state, try to remind ourselves of the love of God, Satan leverages that powerful relationship with disappointment. *Yes, God loves you, but He sure is disappointed in you.* When the demands of life beat us down, these thoughts come easily, and they flood our minds and hearts with more and more shame. We begin to wonder if it is all worth it.

In the pages that follow I want to offer a framework to avoid unnecessary feelings of disappointment, especially feelings of God being disappointed in you. Here are some concepts we will explore in the coming pages:

- How do we project a false identity onto our Father in Heaven and the Savior, which holds us back from a full relationship with Them? (Chapter 1)

- How does disappointment cause us to confuse basic doctrines of the gospel like repentance and grace? (Chapter 2)

- How does a focus on good and bad behavior impede our progress in the gospel of Jesus Christ? (Chapter 3)

IS GOD DISAPPOINTED IN ME?

- How are "I am" the two most powerful words in the English dictionary, and how does Satan primarily use our perceived identity against us? (Chapter 4)

- How can commandments encourage our eternal progress rather than remind us we keep falling short? (Chapter 5)

- Why do we hide our pain from God, and how can we connect with the Savior so He can heal us? (Chapter 6)

- How does shame cause us to hide, numb, and heal our wounds of the heart? (Chapter 7)

- Does unconditional love from God really exist? (Chapter 8)

- How can we perpetuate the flow of grace into our lives by giving more grace to others? (Chapter 9)

As you continue into the pages of this book I hope you feel a sense of overwhelming encouragement. Because that is what the gospel of Jesus Christ is supposed to offer. If you haven't felt that encouragement up to this point in your life, I hope we can get it back on track.

CHAPTER 1

The Projected False God

I recently came across a thought-provoking painting by *Saturday Evening Post* illustrator Richard Sargent. It is laid out like a four-panel comic strip but instead shows four related images. The first image shows a boss scolding an employee for unacceptable work results. The next panel shows that same employee scolding his wife for unacceptable laundry results. The next panel shows that same wife scolding their toddler son for drawing on the walls. The last panel shows that same toddler son scolding the family cat for making a mess of his toys.

These four images perfectly illustrate the journey of shame as transferred from one individual to the next. Shame really has no other course of progress. It can only be transferred person to person or being to being. Shame is the adversary's greatest attack on the hearts of God's children.

Shame is transferred in many scenarios in life, but it takes on additional strength when it is transferred between two loved ones. This happens in the most innocent of circumstances: the parents who spend long nights pushing homework but the result is a less-than-ideal report card; the mother who dreams of her son serving a mission, but then he has zero desire at age eighteen; the parents who want their temple-married children raising their grandchildren in the gospel, but then those children leave the Church completely. Especially between loved ones, shame transfers in the form of disappointment. We have felt disappointment from a parent when we were younger, and later we might experience being that disappointed parent.

Naturally, we assume our Father in Heaven works the same way. We construct in our minds a false God who is constantly shaking His head with folded arms. The more we struggle, the more He turns away, we feel. We can't understand how the children of Israel created and worshipped a false god, but we don't realize we create our own false god in the moment we assume He is disappointed in us.

When we assume God is disappointed in us, even for a moment, we find it harder to feel fully accepted by Him. These interactions leave us feeling rejected and trapped in a paradox: We want to feel accepted by God, but we can't seem to get rid of our weaknesses and sins in order to feel fully accepted. On the flip side, this shame causes us to feel we are not even acceptable enough to ask God for help overcoming our weaknesses. We create a false god by assuming He holds back His acceptance of us until we clean up our own brokenness by ourselves. We then hold back our brokenness from the only Being able to fix it. This vicious cycle causes us to feel trapped and discouraged, and we consider giving up.

Discovering the True God

Jonathan Edwards, a Puritan preacher in the mid-1700s, was known for scaring people into belief by articulating the horror of damnation. In his sermons he painted vivid pictures of a possible fate:

O sinner! Consider the fearful danger you are in: it is a great furnace of wrath, a wide and bottomless pit, full of the fire of wrath, that you are held over in the hand of that God, whose wrath is provoked and incensed as much against you, as against many of the damned in hell.

The God that holds you over the pit of hell, much as one holds a spider, or some loathsome insect over the fire, abhors you, and is dreadfully provoked.

But, alas! instead of one, how many is it likely will remember this discourse in hell! And it would be a wonder, if some that are now present should not be in hell in a very short time, before this year is out.[2]

Jonathan Edwards's wife, Sarah, described herself "feeling so low in grace"[3] because she interpreted God as only condemning, not at all redemptive.

One morning, while her husband was out of town, Sarah's family hosted a visiting preacher by the name of Reverend Peter Reynolds. This reverend offered a morning prayer that struck Sarah. He spoke to God in a way she had never heard before. "I felt an earnest desire," she recalled, "that, in calling on God, he should say, Father, or that he should address the Almighty under that appellation: on which the thought turned in my mind—Why can I say, Father?—Can I now at this time, with the confidence of a child and without the least misgiving of heart, call God my Father?"[4]

At this moment, a Christian woman who thought she understood God's character had, in fact, discovered a new depth to His soul—one that brought feelings of grace and love. She realized the

God she worshipped was not an angry God, after all; rather, she worshipped a Father in Heaven who deeply loved her.

This story gives me pause and excitement. It encourages me to stop and consider the attributes of my Heavenly Father that *I* may be misinterpreting. It brings me to ask myself if I have allowed my life experiences to limit God's true identity in my mind's eye. Is there more profound love I can find from this Immortal Being that could draw me closer to His heart? Am I missing anything He wants me to understand more deeply?

The weight of a "disappointed God" is evident because we have all felt the sting of disappointment from other loved ones in our mortal journey. But is the concept true? Does God see us as disappointments, or is that a lying tactic the adversary uses to convince us to stop trying and to turn away from God? We need to understand God better to understand what emotions and feelings He can experience in His Godlike existence.

How do we do that? There has been much revealed to us about the nature of God. We know that God has a body of flesh and bone. We know He is a separate individual from His Son, Jesus Christ. We know He speaks to His prophets. Because of the blessing of this restored latter-day doctrine, God feels more like our literal Father. He's not just some energy force out in the galaxy that fills us with love. He's a being with eyes and a nose. He has fingernails! He breathes and speaks. He laughs and cries. He can touch us with His hands and express His love through gestures and excitement.

This phenomenal knowledge of God's characteristics is a blessing, but we can also make assumptions that He is more like us mortals than He really is. We still lack much understanding of God's personality, characteristics, and traits. It is easy to project our personality and attributes from this human experience onto His eternal experience.

If God looks and talks like me, He must think and feel like me. It's important to recognize our similarities with God because this brings us closer to Him and invites Him to engage with us. But it is also important not to define every detail or to fill in the divine gaps with our mortal experience.

Suppose my eight-year-old daughter was required to explain my nature, personality, and attributes to a stranger. I'm not confident the stranger would fully understand who I am by listening to my daughter's description. My daughter possesses only a limited understanding of who I am as an individual. As an eight-year-old, she is simply, and sometimes blissfully, unaware of the many complexities of life that have made me who I am. She doesn't fully see all the moments of depression, anxiety, loss, and doubt that I experience in my own life. Even if I tried to explain it to her, that still wouldn't be enough. She must grow and develop and obtain that knowledge and experience grace by grace in her own life.

My daughter living her childhood experience and observing me, her earthly father, is very similar to us living our mortal experience trying to observe and understand our Eternal Father. Just because we might be a parent who is consistently frustrated or disappointed with our children doesn't mean our Father in Heaven is ever frustrated or disappointed with us. We feel we know and understand Him, but we have an eternity ahead of us in which to learn on a much deeper level of His true identity.

Nothing Will Surprise Us More

Someday we will all have the opportunity to understand God to the fullest—all His nuances, character traits, attributes, and personality. Will it be what we expect? President Ezra Taft Benson said, "Nothing is going to startle us more when we pass through the veil to the other side than to realize how well we know our Father and how familiar his face is to us."[5] Won't that be remarkable? To embrace our Eternal Father and then say, *Of course I remember you! You are my Father. How could I have forgotten?* What a beautiful interaction that will be.

The familiarity of His face won't be the only thing that surprises us. We will be amazed at all we forgot about His characteristics, His patience, and His encouraging heart! We will likely be shocked to discover He was never disappointed in us at all. He was always cheering from mortality's sidelines and excited by our progress. We will likely look into His loving eyes and wonder why we wasted so much time hiding from Him in shame. In His presence, we will have no doubt of His love. We will be accepted by Him and receive His embrace without hesitation. President Russell M. Nelson said, "When you begin to catch even a glimpse of how your Heavenly Father sees you and what He is counting on you to do for Him, your life will never be the same."[6]

When that day comes, when we can finally put everything into the correct perspective, we will be amazed at the number of forces assisting us in our mortal experience. We will realize how easily the adversary has convinced us to lay our own snare (Doctrine and Covenants 10:26) and give up. God assumes the best in us, so let's assume the best in God and minimize that postmortal surprise.

He is so good, so loving, so patient, and so encouraging. He's never been disappointed in us!

CHAPTER 2

Godly Disappointment

I have had the opportunity to visit wards and stakes around the country in a fireside setting where I discuss the lack of disappointment in God's character. Often, I am met with some level of skepticism around the topic.

To begin exploring this concept, we must first start with a basic definition of disappointment.

dis·ap·point·ed
/ˌdisəˈpoin(t)əd/

adjective
1. (of a person) sad or displeased because someone or something has failed to fulfill one's hopes or expectations.[7]

Disappointment cannot exist without hopes and expectations. It is natural to think that a parent figure like God must certainly have hopes and expectations, right? One might say, *Of course our Father in Heaven lives and is motivated by the expectation to "bring to pass [our] immortality and eternal life" (Moses 1:39). Every commandment or covenant He has given to mankind comes with an expectation to follow that commandment or keep that covenant. His expectations are very similar to the expectations that parents have for their children.*

Naturally, we assume God gives us commandments with the expectation that we follow each one. Unfortunately, as mortals, we break commandments all the time and "fall short of the glory of God" (Romans 3:23). Since, we assume, God expects that we will follow all His commandments, and we do not live up to that assumed Godly expectation, we think God, like any other parent, is continuously disappointed by our habit of falling short.

But what we assume about God's hopes and expectations comes, again, from our own limited mortal experience.

From our mortal perspective, hope is a phenomenal concept. This principle makes it possible to progress toward our Father in Heaven. "How is it that ye can attain unto faith, save ye shall have hope?" (Moroni 7:40). As mortals, we need the concept of hope to begin relying on the incredible gift of the Atonement of Jesus Christ. We are encouraged to have a "firm hope [in Jesus Christ] that [we] shall one day rest from all our afflictions" (Alma 34:41). We must first *hope* He can heal us before He can heal us. We need hope, and we experience expectations in our simple mortal understanding.

But God does not have hope or expectation in us.

How can this be? How can a parent, even a Godly parent, not hope that His children will return to Him and expect them to follow His commandments?

He doesn't because He is *beyond* hope and expectations.

God does not have hope; He has perfect knowledge. He does not have *expectations* in us; He has *expectancy* in the power of His Son's

IS GOD DISAPPOINTED IN ME?

Atonement. He doesn't hope that it works out; He *knows* that it will work, and He has an *expectancy* that it will. Just like when we face east in the early morning, we don't expect that the sun will rise; we have an expectancy that it will. We would never wonder or worry that today was the day it didn't happen. It will happen! Every day.

There is an ongoing theological debate about what it means for God to be all knowing. Does that mean He knows every detail of every result that will ever happen? Does He know that you will order ham on your sandwich today rather than salami? Does He know what team will win the World Series next year? This book is not meant to fully unpack the concept of what "all knowing" really means in the context of how our Eternal God thinks.

Suffice it to say that, when it comes to the effectiveness of Jesus Christ's Atonement in saving mankind, God has a full knowledge that it worked and it is done. "He has all wisdom, and all power, both in heaven and in earth" (Mosiah 4:9). He gives us commandments but also knows we will break those commandments. When we do break those commandments, His expectancy of our success doesn't allow Him to be disappointed because His Son has put in place redemption that will allow us to try again and overcome sin. Why would He waste emotion on disappointment or broken expectations? His perfect knowledge enables Him to set that aside and love us completely, wherever we are in mortality.

As mortals this concept is hard to fathom because we continually struggle with limited knowledge and expectations in life. We have a certain level of expectations for those around us, especially our loved ones, and we have limited knowledge of how those expectations will turn out. When our loved ones make choices that shatter our expectations, we feel disappointment. The more expectations

17

we have, the more disappointment we experience when it doesn't work. We assume God is experiencing the same process with us, but God isn't wrestling with expectation and limited knowledge. He has unlimited knowledge and, therefore, full expectancy.

To fully understand this concept of expectation versus expectancy, let me take you back to September 2019. I was out of state at a leadership retreat that took me off the grid—I had no internet connection or cable TV. I am a huge BYU football fan, and there was a big game that weekend—the BYU Cougars were playing the Tennessee Volunteers. Tennessee ranked well nationally, and I was interested to see how my favorite players would line up against them. Since I was off the grid, I missed the game but intended to watch a recording when I returned home. It would have been difficult to avoid knowing the final score during my travels home, so when I got cell phone coverage, I looked up the final score and was pleased to see that BYU had somehow overcome Tennessee in overtime. Before I knew it, I was at home reviewing the game. I noticed I enjoyed watching this particular football game more than others—I was not experiencing my typical frustration or anxiety, because I already knew the final score. Sure, some of my favorite players were dropping passes and losing yardage, but I was "all-knowing" and had complete expectancy in the outcome of the game. No matter what mistakes the players made, I was never disappointed. I knew exactly how it would end. This feeling of zero disappointment was impressive, especially in the final moments of regulation when BYU was seemingly losing the game, with only eighteen seconds remaining. The team had eighty yards to go for a touchdown and at least forty-five yards to have a chance at a game-tying field goal. Nevertheless, there I sat, feeling zero anxiety but still leaning in to see how the impressive ending manifested itself.

When our Father in Heaven watches us struggle in mortality, how can He begin to be disappointed when He knows how the game is won? He has set the score, and we were put on the winning side thousands of years ago by His Beloved Son, Jesus Christ. Yes, of course, we will sin in this life. All of us will drop several commandments as they are passed to us. Some of us will even feel beyond saving, as if we have left the field of play altogether. Elder Jeffrey R. Holland said, "The future of this world has long been declared; the final outcome between good and evil is already known. There is absolutely no question as to who wins because the victory has already been posted on the scoreboard. The only really strange thing in all of this is that we are still down here on the field trying to decide which team's jersey we want to wear!"[8]

Christ secured your winning jersey long ago. There's never been a temptation for God to be disappointed. Your life will not be won in the final seconds; it was won long before you were born.

Repentance Isn't a *Part* of the Gospel; It *Is* the Gospel

Because mistakes, judgment, and stigma dominate this imperfect, mortal world, the repentance process can feel like it comes with a scarlet letter. We often feel this perceived judgment when the mistakes we make are embarrassing, shameful, or feel uncommon. It's evident to everyone in mortality that we are imperfect—we make many mistakes every day. However, the feeling of disappointment gets its fuel when we begin to believe Satan's lie that we sin like nobody else, or our life is more out of control than others'. We see others living the gospel, and, from our perspective, they do it with much more grace and less effort. Admiring other families in the pews on Sunday causes us to wonder what they know that we don't. *How do those parents get to church on time with their children looking like they stepped out of a* Liahona *magazine?* We understand the list of gospel principles discussed in Sunday School but wonder if we are missing a hidden secret about the gospel that suddenly makes life easy. The gospel promises us happiness and peace and great blessings, but day-to-day, we feel like we are barely succeeding at living the gospel.

What we easily forget is that we live the gospel when we repent. Repentance is at the purest level of Christ's doctrine. The scriptures teach us, "Behold, this is my doctrine—whosoever repenteth and cometh unto me, the same is my church" (Doctrine and Covenants 10:67). Or, as Nephi said, "as many of [us] as will repent are the covenant people of the Lord" (2 Nephi 30:2).

Joseph Smith taught, "The fundamental principles of our religion are the testimony of the Apostles and Prophets, concerning Jesus Christ, that He died, was buried, and rose again the third day, and ascended into heaven; and all other things which pertain to our religion are only appendages to it."[9] We might be able to classify the welfare program, indexing, youth basketball, and tithing as appendages of the gospel—but not repentance. Repentance isn't just a nice "side program" to be used when needed, as if it were a fire extinguisher behind glass that is only used during spiritual emergencies. Since it is a result of the Atonement of Jesus Christ, repentance is the core of the doctrine. Repentance is the process of *becoming* like our Father in Heaven through the power of Jesus Christ.

With repentance being at the very center of how God Himself defines the gospel, He is never disappointed when we have to use it. He cheers us on every time we repent because, by repenting, we are quite literally living His gospel. "Repentance isn't His backup plan in the event we might fail. Repentance is His plan, knowing that we will."[10]

IS GOD DISAPPOINTED IN ME?

God Has An Expectancy That We Will Sin

One of the most significant purposes of this mortal experience is to return to the presence of our loving Heavenly Father. But have you ever considered why we left His presence in the first place, when we are only trying to get back? Why didn't we just stay in His warm embrace and avoid the struggle of this mortal experience? God had a more excellent plan to develop us as His children. He knew that the temptations, trials, and tribulations of this world would strengthen us to become more like Him. The more we are like Him, the deeper the relationship we can have with Him—and the deeper the relationship we have with Him, the more profound a love we will discover through it.

God expects us to fall into temptation, to mess up, and to make regrettable actions. "We will all be tempted; no man is free from temptation. The adversary will use every means possible to deceive us."[11] Of course, God never encourages us to sin or wants us to sin, because we don't grow by sinning—we grow through repenting, living His gospel, and gaining the strength to face the temptation the next time it shows up. In the famous words of C. S. Lewis, "Only those who try to resist temptation know how strong it is. . . . You find out the strength of a wind by trying to walk against it, not by lying down."[12] I would add that you also understand the strength of the wind when it has already knocked you down, when you are trying to stand up again.

To manifest disappointment, one must have an expectation and a lack of knowledge, and God has always known that we would sin in mortality. Of course, Satan wants us to feel the shaming weight of disappointment when we sin because we are less likely to turn to our Father in Heaven for help. We suddenly become soaked in regret, and Satan tells us to run and hide. So that is what we do: we hide from our family, our spouse, our neighbors, and, most regrettably, we hide from God.

He didn't only expect us to sin in the simplest of ways, with white lies and an occasional slip of the tongue; He knew some of His children would fall into intense addictions, commit deep deception, and even break sacred covenants through infidelity. We see that we have made a mess of things, and there is nothing God wants more than for us to turn to Him, recognize the mess we have created, and say, *Help! What do I do next to get out of this and become more like You? Will You help me stand up again? How can I live Your gospel and grow through repentance?*

This process can be painful. When sin has been committed and so much damage has been done to our lives and the lives around us it can seem impossible to stand up again, to repent, and to find God's encouragement. It is a beautiful journey and a process of joy for not only us but for our shepherd, "our Good Shepherd, [who] finds joy in seeing His diseased sheep progress toward healing."[13] He Himself has spoken of the "joy [that] shall be in heaven over one sinner that repenteth, more than over ninety and nine just persons, which need no repentance" (Luke 15:7).

Sometimes personal disappointment can show up in ways unrelated to sin. We might fail to study before a big final exam, or we might find we continuously walk in late to sacrament meeting. These actions are not breaking a specific commandment, but we can still feel disappointed in ourselves and assume God feels disappointed in us for not doing better. I am the youngest of four children in my family, and all of my older siblings appeared to excel academically. My brother, just older than me, earned straight As all through high school, was the valedictorian of his graduating class,

IS GOD DISAPPOINTED IN ME?

and earned a full-ride scholarship to BYU. No matter how hard I tried, however, I ended up with an average GPA, a below-average ACT score, and three rejection letters from BYU. I was beyond disappointed in myself and quickly assumed God felt the same disappointment in me.

In a world where it is so easy to compare your shortcomings to others' successes it is easy to drown in personal disappointment and project that same feeling onto God. The truth is, He knew you would fall short and wouldn't measure up perfectly to His Son, Jesus Christ—whether through frustrating mortal limitations (like my BYU story) or through sin itself. But that knowledge doesn't make you any less precious to Him. That's why He so eagerly offered His Son to us. That's why the Son so eagerly gave the sacrifice. He is all knowing of your sins, both past, present, and future. And still, He is on your side cheering you on. Keep going!

Grace and Disappointment

"I glory in plainness; I glory in truth; I glory in my Jesus, for he hath redeemed my soul from hell" (2 Nephi 33:6). I love considering the grace of Jesus Christ. His Atonement is beautiful, and the knowledge of it feeds my soul and gives me unlimited hope. I love the concept of the verb *to proffer*. It is a word we have sung hundreds of times during the preparation of the sacrament in the hymn *I Stand All Amazed* (*Hymns*, no. 193): "I stand all amazed at the love Jesus offers me, / Confused at the grace that so fully he proffers me."

I once heard Brad Wilcox masterfully expound upon the word "proffer" in the context of grace. He defined "proffer" as "proactively offering."[14] Jesus wants us to be swaddled in His grace, and we are strengthened by it. Consider the suffering and time that Christ put into His Atonement. He earned it, and He wants us to use it!

His grace is so enormous, so infinite, so available to us, that He is never disappointed when we partake of it. In fact, it is impossible for grace and disappointment to coexist. Can you imagine a heaven where God, after sending us to mortality, is suddenly surprised when His children start sinning and now can't return to His presence? Did God suddenly scramble to find Jesus Christ? Did God explain to Jesus that He didn't mean for Him to have to suffer and save mankind? Was God surprised that when people started to sin, He would *have* to send His Only Begotten Son down to suffer for all mankind? Of course not! The Atonement and sacrifice of God's Son was never His backup plan. It was never a disappointing request for Him to save irresponsible mankind by sending His Son. The Atonement of Jesus Christ was "prepared from the foundation of the world for all mankind" (Mosiah 4:7).

God is never frustrated or disappointed when we have to partake of the Atonement. We never show up to church and expect them not to administer the sacrament, assuming everyone present had a perfect week. The bishop never has to stretch time to fit that sacred ordinance into the agenda. On Sunday, the sacrament *is* the agenda. It's the focus of the meeting. We don't leave it in the corner of the chapel just in case someone needs it; we summon young deacons to "proactively" bring it to us—to each individual.

It's impossible; grace and disappointment cannot coexist. Jesus did the work—He suffered and hung on a cross, covering the payment for all sin and weakness that you experience. As a representation of that sacrifice, He metaphorically places pieces of bread and cups of water on a tray each week. He metaphorically brings that tray wherever you are in life and offers it to you to partake.

IS GOD DISAPPOINTED IN ME?

When you reach out and eat or drink, He never winces with disappointment that *once again* you need to repent. You partaking of His sacrament makes Him happy—happy that His sacrifice continues to work and that you are choosing to accept it and use it for its intended purpose. If we ever feel like God is disappointed that we need His grace again through the sacrament, we can immediately recognize that thought as coming from Satan. Reject it and take His grace—it's for you. God and Jesus Christ find joy in your growth from it.

The Disappointed God in the Scriptures

During the spring of 1828, Joseph Smith was focused on translating The Book of Mormon with his dedicated friend Martin Harris. They had a large portion of the manuscript completed, known as the 116 pages. Because of Martin's dedication to Joseph when so many individuals were not offering their support, Martin pled with Joseph to allow him to take the manuscript home to his wife and relatives to validate the important work they were doing. After several petitions to the Lord, Joseph was allowed to let Martin take the manuscript.

The 116 pages of the manuscript were stolen and never found. Imagine the anguish that Martin must have felt telling Joseph the manuscript was gone. Imagine the anger and disappointment Joseph must have felt hearing the news. Martin said, "Oh, I have lost my soul!"[15] Considering that Martin and Joseph were doing a critical work, you can imagine the fear they must have felt for disrupting the work of God with a now seemingly foolish request to show off the manuscript.

This historic tragedy resulted in what we now call Doctrine and Covenants section 3. Any casual reader can review that section and think, *Wow, God is disappointed and is giving it to Joseph.* When read in a specific tone, passages in section 3 can easily sound like an angry and disappointed lecture a parent would give to a foolish teenager:

> HOW OFT YOU HAVE TRANSGRESSED THE COMMANDMENTS AND THE LAWS OF GOD, AND HAVE GONE ON IN THE PERSUASIONS OF MEN!!! FOR, BEHOLD, YOU SHOULD NOT HAVE FEARED MAN MORE THAN GOD!!! ALTHOUGH MEN SET AT NAUGHT THE COUNSELS OF GOD, AND DESPISE HIS WORDS—YET YOU SHOULD HAVE BEEN FAITHFUL; AND HE WOULD HAVE EXTENDED HIS ARM AND SUPPORTED YOU AGAINST ALL THE FIERY DARTS OF THE ADVERSARY; AND HE WOULD HAVE BEEN WITH YOU IN EVERY TIME OF TROUBLE!!! (verses 6–8)

In the official source of the scriptures, you will find that the words are not in all caps, and there are no exclamation marks; however, that's how most readers interpret them. We assume that God is using some type of loud, mean "dad voice" that is showering shame down on Joseph. However, if you were to ask a sweet grandmother to read these same verses of scripture in her most encouraging voice, it would sound like loving correction and encouragement. The verses that follow after verse 8 contain messages of sincere love and hope, reminding Joseph that "God is merciful" and that Joseph is "still chosen" and "called to the work" (Doctrine and Covenants 3:10).

IS GOD DISAPPOINTED IN ME?

Are the scriptures full of a disappointed God? We can point to other verses in scripture with strong language that make it easy to interpret God as very disappointed:

"Repent, lest I come out and smite them with a curse, and they die." (Moses 7:10)

When we rebel we "provoke [God] in anger." (Jacob 1:8)

"I, the Lord, am not well pleased with the inhabitants of Zion." (Doctrine & Covenants 68:31)

"For the wrath of God is revealed from heaven." (Romans 1:18)

"I am not well pleased with many things." (Doctrine and Covenants 60:2).

We must be careful of the assumptions we make about God's character and state of mind when He speaks in the scriptures. We've all misinterpreted the tone of a text message from a loved one, assuming they are raging mad because they left off the wink emoji. Our brain isn't much help here, as it is wired to perceive any level of threat, and, therefore, it often assumes the worst. Let's assume the best intentions—not only with the text messages we receive, but also with the scriptures we read. We worship a loving God, so let's assume He has a loving tone in the words He speaks through scripture.

In Doctrine and Covenants section 3, before the famous "dad voice" verses we just reviewed, God makes a profound statement

27

about His lack of disappointment. It's as if He wanted to make clear to Joseph that He wasn't disappointed but simply wanted to give correction and guidance:

> The works, and the designs, and the purposes of God *cannot be frustrated*, neither can they come to naught. For *God doth not walk in crooked paths*, neither doth he turn to the right hand nor to the left, neither doth he vary from that which he hath said, therefore his paths are straight, and *his course is one eternal round. Remember, remember that it is not the work of God that is frustrated, but the work of men.* (Doctrine and Covenants 3:1–3; emphasis added)

The Lord was testifying to Joseph of His strength as the Eternal Creator. God never threatened Joseph with the loss of his soul. Even the chosen prophet couldn't frustrate the work of God. God simply reminded Joseph of His omniscience and omnipotence. After this experience Joseph was better prepared to trust his Father in Heaven.

Confusing Correction with Disappointment

When my friend Dani was fifteen years old, she was on a competitive girls' soccer team preparing for a tournament in China. She was a teenager and had a lot going on. One day during practice, she was having a hard time getting her head in the game and giving a high level of effort. Dani's coach picked up on this and called her out on her lack of mental stamina. Immediately, Dani felt defensive. Her coach had the nerve to be disappointed in her efforts. She cynically apologized, explaining that she wasn't a machine and she couldn't be at one-hundred-percent capacity every moment of every day. Dani's coach saw an opportunity to give direction. He pulled her aside and gave her some perspective that she has never forgotten: "Dani, I know you are going to have off days, but as your coach, it is my responsibility to make you aware of when you are straying from the path of success. If you are willing to show up at your peak performance level, even on the hard days, I'll do my best to train you, even if it means discomfort and facing hard truths" (Dani Hayes, personal communication with author).

What Dani remembers most about this experience was how much love her coach showed her. She knew she had a coach that cared about her and only wanted to see her discover the elite soccer player she could become.

There is always a moment in a great sports movie when the pressure is on. At that moment, the coach gets at eye level with the players and shares the hard truths the team needs to hear to overcome the weaknesses in their game. Don't we all want a coaching relationship with God? "Behold, happy is the man whom God correcteth: therefore despise not thou the chastening of the Almighty" (Job 5:17).

When we interpret God's correction as disappointment rather than coaching, it leaves us vulnerable to the adversary and his attempts at damaging our identity and self-worth. When Dani first responded to her coach, she was making it about her self-worth. *Maybe I should just quit the team if the coach doesn't think I'm good enough to play or if he thinks I need to be at one hundred percent all the time.* Her coach knew she was good enough to play and even great enough to excel at that level.

Dani later shared how this experience helped her understand God's coaching in her life:

This interaction with my coach was the first time in my life that I ever realized that having someone displeased or disappointed in me is not an indication of my worthiness. I think too often we measure our self-worth based on whether or not we are living up to other people's expectations or even God's expectations (assuming He has expectations). At that moment, the lesson my coach wanted me to learn was that he wasn't there to measure my value or my self-worth. He was showing up every day to guide me—I was already qualified. He was a compass, not a measuring stick. This is how it is with our Heavenly Father. Because He knows the beginning from the end, because He is our Creator, He has infinite love for us. He is there to help us course-correct when necessary. Heavenly Father knows that we can't be perfect in this life. Therefore, our eternal worth is not diminished when we are imperfect; that is part of the plan. (Dani Hayes, personal communication with author)

Just because God never experiences disappointment in us doesn't mean, however, that we're immune from uncomfortable feelings. Some Christians interpret God as purely love and rarely consider that such love may feel uncomfortable when God steps in as a coach and offers us correction. When we mess up or point our life down the wrong path, God isn't going to shrug it off. He's going to figure out a way to get at eye level with us and remind us of our relationship to Him and the eternal identity He bestowed

IS GOD DISAPPOINTED IN ME?

in us. We need the strength that comes through a relationship with an Eternal Coach Who will give us the hard truth even when we don't want to hear it. Only God knows the potential in each of us, and He is, therefore, the only one who can help us reach it.

Desiring a Disappointed God

In our Latter-day Saint culture, there is a lot of focus on behaviors, commandments, and righteous habits. Rightly so, since there is so much good that comes from behaving according to God's commandments (chapter 5). Because of this focus, I often see Latter-day Saints cautiously approach the doctrine of grace. They understand that Christ's "grace is sufficient" (2 Corinthians 12:9) and that salvation will only come "because of the righteousness of [our] Redeemer" (2 Nephi 2:3). Some worry that emphasizing grace "too much" might cause people to think, *Why am I trying so hard? Why am I worried about these commandments when, in reality, Christ is the one earning my ticket to heaven?* This concern is understandable, but if someone does interpret grace as a license to be casual with the commandments, they don't understand grace.

The same argument is made when some hear the idea that God has never been disappointed in them, as if hearing such an idea would cause people to be lax in their worship and efforts toward keeping the commandments. Or they might think, *If God is never disappointed in me, what is going to keep me motivated to stay on the covenant path?* We sometimes want a loving God to get mad and disappointed in us, thinking that this parental fear will scare us back to the straight and narrow path. This is the power of shame and disappointment. We probably all have experience seeing our mortal fathers get visually angry to the point that it scared us into

31

conformity. The transfer of shame is effective in motivating us, but it causes us to question if love still remains in those relationships. It is effective, but we end up being afraid and avoid those who motivate through shame. What parent wants that?

When we remove the disappointment from our relationship with our Heavenly Father, it leaves room for more love. The motivation that comes from disappointment (or shame) pales in comparison to the motivation that comes from love. When I consider the love my Father in Heaven has for me, or when I am in those moments where His love envelops me, there is nothing I want to do more than to keep His commandments and to keep trying. I want to become more and more like Him, not because I am scared of Him, but because I am intrigued by His character. I am drawn to learn to love as He loves. Don't be afraid of removing the disappointed God from your life. He is a loving God, ready to encourage you through His beautiful commandments and covenants.

Why Does God Weep?

In Moses 7 Enoch walks with God and is shown many groups of people. He is encouraged to preach to them. This chapter makes references to a portion of God's children that He classifies as "the residue"—"Zion have I blessed but the residue of the people have I cursed" (verse 20). It later says "that the God of heaven looked upon the residue of the people, and he wept" (verse 28).

Then comes my favorite part of this chapter. As God is now weeping, Enoch asks, "How is it that thou canst weep?" (verse 29). Enoch wasn't surprised that God had tear ducts or had the ability to cry, but He was astonished at what was causing Him to weep. "Thou art holy, and from all eternity to all eternity. . . . And were it possible that man could number the particles of the earth, yeah, millions of earths like this, it would not be a beginning to the number of thy creations" (verses 29–30). As if Enoch was saying, *look at all the good You have done to so many millions of people. You have been so merciful and saved so many, yet You weep over this tiny portion or residue of people?*

In this moment, God now has an opening to explain to Enoch just how much He loves all His children, even the residue:

> The Lord said unto Enoch: Behold these thy brethren; *they are the workmanship of mine own hands*, and I gave unto them their knowledge, in the day I created them; and in the Garden of Eden, gave I unto man his agency;
>
> And the fire of mine indignation is kindled against them; and *in my hot displeasure* will I send in the floods upon them, for my fierce anger is kindled against them.
>
> Behold, I am God, Man of Holiness is my name; Man of Counsel is my name; and Endless and Eternal is my name, also.
>
> Wherefore, *I can stretch forth mine hands and hold all the creations which I have made*; and mine eye can pierce them also, and among all the workmanship of mine hands there has not been so great wickedness as among thy brethren.
>
> But behold, their sins shall be upon the heads of their fathers; Satan shall be their father, and misery shall be their doom; and the whole heavens shall weep over them, even all the workmanship of mine hands; wherefore should not the heavens weep, seeing these shall suffer? (Moses 7:32–37)

These verses pierce the heart! They show the raw nature of our Father in Heaven. Here are His people, His workmanship. They are His children, and they have rejected Him after He has tried so hard to reach them. God wants to be their Father, but they are making Satan their father. These children He loves so profoundly have rejected Him and will suffer without His relationship. Of course, God weeps.

Team Residue

This explanation to Enoch is one of a few scriptural experiences that can easily be interpreted as God being disappointed in His children. The Almighty God is weeping over His children! It looks like disappointment, but how could that be? Didn't He know the "residue of His people" were going to reject Him? Yes, of course God knew this would happen, and He isn't weeping because of disappointment; He's weeping because of love. It doesn't matter how many times God watches the Moses 7 tape; He always weeps. Not because He hopes the "residue of his people" won't reject Him this time around, but because He created a plan guaranteed to work, a Savior who already won, and some of His children still gave up and walked off the field. Salvation was there for the taking, and Team Residue rejected it.

It's hard to say who is on Team Residue, but it's definitely not you. The mother who is striving each day to improve but keeps falling short. Is she on Team Residue? Has she given up and walked off the field? No. God has never been disappointed in her. What about the returned missionary who has felt the power of redemption so strongly after teaching it to families in a far-off country but now is trapped in sexual addiction—is he on Team Residue? No. Well, what about the teenager who has to constantly return to the bishop's office after making the same mistake over and over and over again? Is he on Team Residue? No.

All these people are doing their best to stay engaged in the gospel and use the glorious gift of repentance. God wants us to "understand [His] mercies which [He] has bestowed upon [us] because of [His] Son" (Alma 33:16). Christ suffered so much for us and paid an enormous price for our salvation. He never wants us to be reluctant to use it or feel ashamed for having to repent constantly.

We all have days where it feels like we have given up, but your Eternal Coach is helping you. You might have loved ones who seem to have given up, but for all you know, they are just on the sidelines for a moment, walking off a spiritually twisted ankle or catching their breath. Maybe they even think they will never return to the field of redemption. All the while, they have the best Coach in eternity, getting them warmed up and ready to return to the field.

CHAPTER 3

Behaviors versus Heart

Gloria, a young mother, was standing outside a ward member's home with dinner in hand. This visit was one of the many "service opportunities" that the compassionate service leader in her Relief Society asked her to fulfill. The dinner wasn't perfect, but it was what she had the strength to make. She could have done better; in fact, she wondered if falling short invalidated this service opportunity because she *didn't* do more. The longer she stood on the doorstep, the more she convinced herself that she should have done more. Finally, the door opened, and a sweet, older lady greeted Gloria. Her eyes were full of gratitude that Gloria would take the time to bring her a warm meal. Gloria was numb to the appreciation and almost couldn't understand the words of love she was offered. Gloria continued to dwell on how she could have done better. By checking this service box, Gloria only remembered all the other tasks not completed—the school projects, the messy laundry room, the failed date night. She was failing as a Latter-day Saint, and before she knew it, tears of exhaustion rolled down her cheeks. An emotional breakdown unfolded on the porch steps as the concerned and confused ward member looked on.

This emotional breakdown didn't happen suddenly—the pressure had been building for years. Gloria grew up in a traditional, orthodox Latter-day Saint home. Rules and commandments were encouraged but not overly forced. Gloria appreciated her growing testimony and saw herself as a person who was "all in" and never a fence-sitter. She later married in the temple with all the expectations of any young Latter-day Saint wife: she would grow a family, attend church, and see her children flourish in the gospel. But over time, that storybook journey was turning into something entirely different. All the ingredients seemed to be there: She married an incredible man who had a testimony of his own, and their family established consistent family prayer, scripture study, and regular church attendance. Still, when she attended church and listened to others articulate their own gospel experience, it sounded increasingly foreign to her own experience. Her ward members would share, with tears in their eyes, how much they felt God's help in their lives and how they felt overcome with the Spirit each day. Gloria couldn't help but recognize the spiritual hole she felt in her own life. She could only conclude she was doing something wrong. Maybe she wasn't following the gospel equation correctly. Maybe she wasn't doing enough. She was certain God was always disappointed in her.

Hope and Expectations of Behaviors

Like Gloria, we all have certain expectations in life, both for ourselves and our loved ones. At the time of this writing, I have two daughters and one son. I relate so much to my five-year-old son's

IS GOD DISAPPOINTED IN ME?

experience. Just like my five-year-old self, he is determined to become a superhero. He is always up for a sword fight, and he sees the backyard as a world full of adventure. I have so much hope for my son's future. I want to father him in a way that will help him grow into a better man than I am. I can close my eyes and almost see his future unfold. He's going to love having me coach his rec league basketball team. We will practice together for hours on the driveway court to refine his skills, and I'll hopefully see him play on the competitive high school team. He will receive the priesthood and execute his priesthood duties well as we minister to various families together. He'll attend seminary and cherish each new eternal truth he learns. A mission will follow, then temple marriage, and then the opportunity to teach his children in righteousness. In the end, everyone will live happily ever after.

These hopes and ambitions are similar to the hopes and ambitions that any Latter-day Saint father has for his children, but as we all know, our perfect plan for our children doesn't always go according to plan. I am sure Alma the Elder had similar plans for his son, Alma the Younger, to grow and develop in righteousness. He likely felt great disappointment when his son began persecuting God's Church. However, we know how the story ends: Alma the Younger is visited by an angel and has a miraculous change of heart. After being struck dumb by the angel of the Lord for several days, Alma stands and speaks these powerful words:

> For, said he, I have repented of my sins, and have been redeemed of the Lord; behold I am born of the Spirit. And the Lord said unto me: Marvel not that all mankind, yea, men and women, all nations, kindreds,

tongues and people, must be born again; yea, born of God, changed from their carnal and fallen state, to a state of righteousness, being redeemed of God, becoming his sons and daughters. (Mosiah 27:24–25)

He was a "new creature" and encouraged all to become new creatures to inherit the kingdom of God.

Isn't this what we all want for our children? Isn't that what Gloria hoped for as well? We can all recognize that we will face difficult times in life or that our children won't follow the perfect path, but all we want is a conversion experience, leading to a deep change of heart. Elder Spencer J. Condie said, "One of the powerful doctrines of The Book of Mormon is that we can, indeed we must, undergo a mighty change of heart."[16] That was also the message that Christ shared with Nicodemus when He explained, "Ye must be born again" (John 3:7).

Consider who your most earnest prayers are for—maybe one of your children, a brother or sister who has stepped away from the Church, or even a good friend who is questioning their faith and testimony. We want to encourage these individuals toward personal conversion, just like Alma the Elder wanted to do with his son. We wish we had an angel of God on speed dial whom we could summon from heaven to put our loved one in a mighty, heart-changing spiritual coma for several days.

Or maybe we are experiencing our own struggles, like Gloria, and feel exhausted in continually disappointing God. We may feel like we are sabotaging our potential to have the same spiritual experiences our fellow Latter-day Saints seem to be having. We may feel alone, thinking we are the only one with secret doubts and aren't

IS GOD DISAPPOINTED IN ME?

sure how to reconcile them. Perhaps we catch ourselves wondering how everyone else around us has figured out the gospel equation of happiness, and we barely survive each day. Maybe our heart is breaking as we see a loved one push the gospel away from their heart—the same gospel we diligently try to push into our own heart.

When we want to influence ourselves or loved ones toward personal conversion, we typically look toward certain behaviors that will, hopefully, help us or them get back on track. We buy a brand-new scripture journal to reinvest ourselves in the scriptures. We draw up a family schedule that makes family scripture study and prayer a priority. We commit for the ten-thousandth time that today is the last day we will ever struggle with pornography again. I am sure you can think of the behavior-focused efforts you have tried to "get life back on track" or to manifest a change of heart for a loved one. The point being, we typically try to control life and manifest a new change of heart through behaviors. But naturally, we find that these behaviors—which we have likely attempted before—lead us back to the same frustration of seemingly not measuring up. We assume a change of behaviors will lead to a change of heart when, in reality, we need to set aside behaviors for a time and focus completely on the heart.

Behavior First, Heart Second

As parents, the desperation of personal conversion for our children seems heavy. We feel it is our duty to control their environments, habits, schedules, and day-to-day experiences so they reach personal conversion. We can't help but turn up the dial on righteous behaviors first, with the hope that these actions will begin to change their hearts and lead to deep conversion. We are desperate for our children to experience spiritual health in these difficult modern times, and so we commit to formulating a life full of righteous habits. Weekly church attendance is the law of the land. Parents might start to rigorously scrutinize their teenager's music selections for unclean language and inappropriate content. They turn internet filters to their highest settings. Missing family scripture study at 6 a.m. is followed by the strongest of punishments. In these moments of gospel instruction, they go for the hard sell by highlighting stories of conversion. With their teenagers present, they flip open to Alma 29 and try to project the feeling "O, that I were an angel" onto their children's hearts, hoping these verses will penetrate into their souls. They can't help but flip over to the words of Paul, an Apostle who tried the rebellious life and then later proclaimed after his conversion, "For to be carnally minded is death; but to be spiritually minded is life and peace" (Romans 8:6).

We hope this hyper-focus on righteous behaviors will cause our loved ones to sound like King Benjamin's people: "O have mercy, and apply the atoning blood of Christ that we may receive forgiveness of our sins, and our hearts may be purified; for we believe in Jesus Christ, the Son of God" (Mosiah 4:2).

My eight-year-old girl and five-year-old son are in a very impressionable stage of life. As we gather in their bedroom at bedtime for family prayer, it isn't uncommon to hear my five-year-old begin to pray to the Almighty God in a silly voice that seems only fit for a Muppet. He sees this as some sort of comedy routine to garner a laugh from his older sister. As his father, if I don't correct this bad form, my son might grow up disrespecting prayer, never understand the reverence of the gospel, and may even dismiss serving a mission later in life. He'll then teach his kids bad form, and then my posterity will forget how to pray altogether! In the past I have typically turned on my dad voice and corrected the inappropriate nature of his prayer. Or, if he isn't kneeling how I like, or even lying on the floor, I rebuke him so that he never forgets the appropriate behaviors that show reverence during family prayer. It took me a while to realize that when I make prayer all about behavior, my children miss the message of prayer altogether.

For many, this *behaviors-first* approach works in a controlled environment. Teenagers can seem to be excelling in life, getting good grades, and enjoying seminary. It's easy to assume the formula is working.

Righteousness + Consistency = Change of Heart

So when we have a child who begins to rebel, we assume the answer is to simply turn up the righteous behaviors by setting stricter rules and offering overwhelming praise for positive spiritual behaviors at home or at church. More and more mandates are put in place, and disappointed looks are distributed in order to get the desired behaviors.

These behavior-focused attempts happen on a personal level as well. Life gets hard, and we aren't sure why trials are cropping up in our life, so we immediately reflect on our behaviors: *Have I been reading my scriptures enough? Maybe my prayers should be more sincere? I'll double my temple attendance this month and see if that will get things back on track.* Though all these behaviors seem reasonable, we often miss the purpose of doing them. We see scripture study, prayer, and temple attendance as only part of the giant prosperity gospel gumball machine in heaven—we put in "righteous behaviors," and out come blessings. God never intended for the gospel to be a math equation, and if we keep seeing it that way, we might end up having an emotional breakdown on our neighbor's porch.

When we build relationships on behavior (either between our children and us or between God and us), we begin to define ourselves by our behavior. Our "righteous" children begin to think they are loved because of their righteous behavior. Our "rebellious" children begin to believe they are not loved because of their bad behavior. Or we, ourselves, begin to think God is continuously disappointed in us, wondering when we are ever going to figure out how to perform in mortality. We often forget that there is a sly adversary behind the scenes, slowly dripping corruption into our behavior equation. He knows we have focused so much on behaviors that we have missed opportunities to show love to our loved ones or that we have assumed the absence of God's love, leaving us vulnerable. Satan quietly begins to tie behaviors to identity and worthiness. He knows "that the time shall come when it shall no more be expedient [for your children] to keep [your parental] law" (Mosiah 13:27), and your "controlled environment" will come to an end when your children move out of your protected home. They will have to face spiritual warfare in the real world without your behavior-focused structure keeping them in line. Parenting shame may work in a structured context, but it will fail children in the real world.

When we start our relationship with God focused on behavior, we run the risk of conversion never taking root, because "salvation doth not come by the law alone" (Mosiah 13:28). Conversion happens in the heart, not in the hands.

Heart First, Behavior Second

When we put behaviors second, it is easy to feel uncomfortable and wonder what the correct approach is. Or, as one father said to me, "You think I should just give up on my child?" Should you let your children run wild and figure life out on their own terms?

A focus on behaviors is not overrated. Behaviors are essential; in fact, they are crucial in our journey to become like our Heavenly Father. Our journey in the gospel begins to break down, however, when we focus on behaviors before heart. President Ezra Taft Benson said, "The Lord works from the inside out. The world works from the outside in. . . . The world would mold men by changing their environment. Christ changes men, who then change their environment. The world would shape human behavior, but Christ can change human nature."[17]

The Lord didn't wait until Alma the Younger began to show righteous behavior before he changed his heart—He changed his heart (by sending an angel), and then the righteous behavior followed. God didn't wait until Saul was on the road to righteousness—He found him on the road to Damascus, changed his heart, and righteous behavior followed. Jesus didn't seek disciples in the synagogue where Pharisees had proven themselves according to their behaviors—He found disciples in fishing boats, changed their hearts, and righteous behaviors followed. After hearing the words of King Benjamin, his people commented on how they first felt "a mighty change in us, or in our hearts" and then wanted to observe righteous behaviors—"we have no more disposition to do evil, but to do good continually" (Mosiah 5:2).

Elder Hans T. Boom said, "We all know where we can do better. There is no need to repeatedly remind each other, but there is a need to love and minister to each other and, in doing so, provide a *climate of willingness to change.*"[18] All we can do in our life and in the lives of others is create a "climate of willingness to change." The reality is, we can't force anyone to have a conversion experience by beating them with the stick of behaviors. It doesn't matter how many times I tell my five-year-old to sit up, fold his arms, and pray like he means it. I can never force conversion on him through these behaviors. As Nephi said (and Elder Bednar has taught so masterfully), the "Holy Ghost carrieth [the message] *unto* the hearts of the children of men" (2 Nephi 33:1; emphasis added). We can't force conversion *into* the hearts of men. But when we work to create a "climate of willingness to change" by first focusing on the heart, we are much more likely to witness personal conversion. When I first focus on my son's heart by spending time exploring the world of superheroes and joining him in his backyard adventures, or even laughing at his silly Muppet-voice prayer, he is more likely to open his heart in the future when I share spiritual principles, doctrines, and righteous behaviors. He may not behave as I want him to as a five-year-old (and who knows what the teenage years have in store), but if he grows up knowing his father loves his heart, he is more likely to seek my counsel as a sixteen-year-old when his behaviors become more important and more consequential.

This is how God works with his children. Elder Holland has explained it this way:

My brothers and sisters, the first great commandment of all eternity is to love God with all of our heart, might, mind, and strength—that's the first great commandment. But the first great truth of all eternity is that God loves us with all of His heart, might, mind, and strength. That love is the foundation stone of eternity, and it should be the foundation stone of our daily life. Indeed it is only with that reassurance burning in our soul that we can have the confidence to keep trying to improve, keep seeking forgiveness for our sins, and keep extending that grace to our neighbor.[19]

God comes for your heart long before He comes for your behavior. When we assume God is disappointed in our behaviors, we tend to hide our hearts. When we shift our mindset and realize God is pursuing our heart, we give ourselves more grace. We allow Him to work on our heart, knowing that it will help us with our behaviors down the road.

The Adversary Starts with Heart

It's easy to assume that Satan is trying to influence us completely through behaviors. We assume he is continuously following us around, whispering in our ears certain temptations related to behaviors—*Lie to your mother! Skip church today! Go rob a bank!* Assuming the adversary uses the "behavior first, heart second" tactic, we try to combat the destructive behaviors with good behaviors (extra scripture reading, temple attendance, singing a hymn, etc.). We fail to realize that Satan is beating us at our own game.

Alma teaches, "And thus we see how great the inequality of man is because of sin and transgression, and the power of the devil, which comes by the cunning plans which he hath devised to ensnare the *hearts of men*" (Alma 28:13; emphasis added). Instead of convincing us to *behave* in a certain way so that we step into a trap, Satan does something even more effective: He "causes [us] to catch [ourselves] in [our] own [trap]" (Doctrine and Covenants 10:26). While we focus on behaviors, Satan focuses on the heart, which naturally leads to bad behaviors. He knows that our heart is tied to personal identity and shame. If he can convince us to believe we are bad people with bad hearts, he can take the month off and watch us step into our own trap. Overwhelmed by shame, we seek out sin on our own. Trapped in this lie, we are convinced that God is disappointed in us, which only adds fuel to this vicious cycle.

To better understand this approach, let me lay out a framework that can help all of us better understand how we trap ourselves and how we can more effectively stimulate conversion and sanctification in our own life and in the lives of our loved ones.

The Gospel Continuum

In a strong religious culture, it's easy to get overwhelmed by a focus on behaviors when we have so many commandments, policies, rules, and honor codes. Many begin to feel exhausted by all the required behaviors and even feel jaded by their religious experience because they perceive it as all about *do, do, do.* For some people, this hyperfocus on behaviors doesn't necessarily cause them to reject the gospel altogether, but after feeling the overwhelming love of God they may start to dismiss the need for righteous behaviors. *Why do we focus on all these silly rules? The gospel is just about love.* An overwhelming

IS GOD DISAPPOINTED IN ME?

feeling of love and acceptance can make some wonder, *Why the demand for behaviors? God accepts me, and that's enough.*

However, the gospel isn't just about love; rather, the gospel *begins* with love. There is so much more God is offering us. He wants to see us grow and develop to become more like Him. He can't limit His gospel to love and hope we somehow grow, change, and develop. He uses love to motivate us to start our journey. As we offer our heart to God each day we can feel His infinite love and acceptance. This will motivate us to become like Him. Some may see commandments as *silly religious rules* that once felt restrictive but that now become a pathway to becoming more like our Hero in Heaven.

A model called the Gospel Continuum illustrates the collaborative influence that heart and behavior have on each other. It helps us step away from the idea that the gospel is an equation with inputs and outputs and see the gospel experience as more of a flow system, with rhythm and momentum. This type of system better facilitates a journey of repentance, progression, conversion, and personal development. Love becomes dependent on behavior, and behavior becomes dependent on love. These two concepts working together in our life can have a dramatic effect on our discipleship.

Think of the Gospel Continuum as a model for how we experience the gospel of Jesus Christ. We start in nursery, learning mainly about God's love for us. We sing songs focused on love and identity—that's why we all know every word to the Primary song "I Am a Child of God" (*Children's Songbook*, 2–3). As we mature in the gospel, we reach for the temple by refining our behaviors and complying with behavior-focused temple recommend questions. We refine our behaviors to be prepared for more dynamic covenants that will help us grow in new ways—not to earn God's love but, rather, to *learn His identity*. As individuals in this Gospel Continuum, it's as if we are on a pendulum that starts at the heart. As we grow and learn in the gospel, feeling more and more of Christ's graceful acceptance, we progress higher and higher on the heart side of the continuum until we are ready to swing toward the behavior side with much greater momentum.

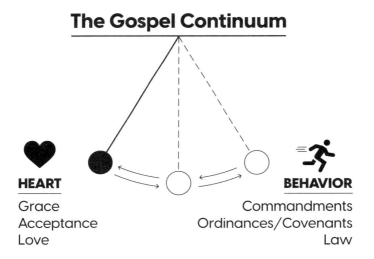

This initial focus on heart and love is as much for the old as it is for the young. We don't graduate from love and never go back once we master the behaviors. We are constantly swinging from side to side as needed. The momentum we get from receiving God's love gives us the momentum or strength to swing to the other side of the continuum and engage more effectively with righteous behaviors. In turn, this allows us to swing back to love with greater force. It's a continual pendulum that swings between love and law, nurturing

IS GOD DISAPPOINTED IN ME?

those who are new to the gospel and others who have been engaged in the gospel most of their life. If we get stuck on the love side of the continuum, where it feels most comfortable, we miss out on the power of behaviors that help sanctify us to become something greater. Without the context of this continuum, we run the risk of assuming the gospel is only one-sided. We either apply the gospel as purely love in an effort to remove pressure and shame, or we only apply the gospel through behaviors, hoping to fix all our problems through righteous-behavior checklists.

My friend Tom's experience of returning to the Church while living in New Canaan, Connecticut, is an excellent example of how this continuum of the gospel can create a climate of willingness to change. I had the opportunity to interview Tom, his bishop, and his stake president for a *Leading Saints* podcast episode. Tom grew up in the Church in a faithful, orthodox family. He knew at a young age that he was gay. This part of his identity led him to leave the Church in the 1980s and live for several decades outside of Church membership. Tom began a relationship with a partner that lasted for many years. Over the course of decades out of the Church, Tom increasingly felt a spiritual nudge to come back. He found his local ward in Connecticut and began attending. Bishop Larson noticed Tom consistently sitting in the back of the chapel each week, and when Tom asked to visit with him the bishop invited Tom over to his home to get to know him better. During that initial interaction, Tom told Bishop Larson his story and explained that he was in a same-sex relationship. Bishop Larson openly invited Tom and his partner to attend church. He never mentioned any behaviors, only an invitation of belonging. This conversation started an inspiring relationship between Tom, his bishop, and President Checketts, the local stake president. President Checketts and his wife extended invitations to Tom and his partner to join them for dinner and began to create an authentic friendship with both of them, never harping on any disapproving behaviors.

Tom had been attending church for about five years, getting to know many of the wonderful Latter-day Saints in his ward. They welcomed him each week with love and friendship. After so many years of attending church, it would be tempting for a bishop to begin prodding an individual like Tom toward the behavioral side of the continuum by pressuring behavioral changes in his life. As I interviewed Bishop Larson and President Checketts, they clarified that the best way to lead Tom in this journey was to let him set the pace of his increasing engagement and to focus on relationships before commandments—or, in other words, focus on heart rather than on behavior. The following year, President Checketts invited Tom over to his home each Saturday morning to sit and study the gospel together. There was no passive-aggressive focus on specific doctrines that might convince Tom to change his behavior; President Checketts invited Tom to select and research the topics and doctrines he wanted to better understand, and they simply invited the Spirit into that interaction and were both sanctified by it. In one of those conversations, Tom invited President Checketts to ask him the questions in a temple recommend interview. When Tom answered affirmatively the question about living the law of chastity, President Checketts jokingly said, "Let's go fill the font!" Nothing had happened overnight, but little by little, Tom had made steps to prepare himself to be baptized once again in the gospel. Tom made dramatic changes in his behavior—initially in small ways, and over time in quite significant ones. He was rebaptized into the gospel, and later his temple blessings were restored.[20]

IS GOD DISAPPOINTED IN ME?

Back and Forth on the Continuum

One might be confused by the swinging-pendulum model of the Gospel Continuum. Tom's experience seems very linear, as he was met with love and then later took on more righteous behaviors. Again, this continuum of gospel living is not a one-way street. The Lord is continually encouraging us to return to various parts of this continuum, hoping we find a new *climate of willingness to change.* Sometimes, as we attend the temple, the Lord directs our mind toward specific behaviors we could work on because He knows we can find deeper sanctification in those efforts. Other times the Lord might swing us back toward the heart side of the continuum by inviting us to focus on a specific gospel song or hymn rather than engaging in the behavior of scripture study. You may not *learn* anything intellectually about the gospel on those particular days, but maybe God is wanting you to put aside a particular behavior that day so you can be reminded of His love and full acceptance of you regardless of your behaviors. God will engage with you on different parts of the continuum depending on your state of mind, life circumstances, and where He would like to nourish and heal you.

In my personal life, I notice some days I need a long, deep (behavior-focused) scripture-study session using scriptural commentaries, Hebrew translations, and a fresh pen for some serious writing in my scripture journal. Other days I simply need a quiet moment alone listening to spiritual music to remind me of God's love. Occasionally I need a love-filled Elder Holland talk, and other times I need President Oaks telling me where I am falling short on the covenant path. The pendulum-like nature of the continuum creates momentum in our lives going both ways. The more we find love and acceptance from God (moving higher up the love side of the continuum), the more momentum we have to swing toward righteous behaviors. And then, ideally, we can build upon righteous behaviors and use that momentum to swing back into God's love and acceptance in order to recharge and swing back. The continuum is most effective when there is movement. It is as if we are dancing on this continuum, back and forth, up and down, discovering deeper love, and then swinging back to refine our behaviors.

The Gravity of Grace and One-Way Momentum

With any basic pendulum, you can build momentum by pushing it either way because the main pull of gravity is down. However, the gravitational pull of the Gospel Continuum pendulum pulls toward love. I call this the gravity of grace. Only by surrendering to this gravity of grace and pushing toward the love side of the continuum will we begin to gain momentum. As discussed earlier, we cannot try to build momentum by pushing ourselves or others toward behavior and expect them to naturally swing toward love. We can't earn it through behaviors; we can only receive it through love. Much like how God encourages us, if we expect behaviors to improve, we can only encourage others or ourselves toward love and acceptance. The continuum will lock up if we try to only push toward behaviors. Once momentum has begun, deeper engagement with behaviors then has the power to propel us toward deeper love; but we can never start by pushing toward behavior.

In a Sunday School class, it is typical to hear individuals respond to certain questions with what is often referred to as the "Sunday School answers" or the "seminary answers." *In order to show faith, what do we do? Read your scriptures, go to church, pray, etc.* All behavior-focused. Instead of these behavior-focused scripted answers, the correct answer is always, *We must first realize we are*

IS GOD DISAPPOINTED IN ME?

loved and completely accepted by Jesus Christ. Once we accept His grace in that way, we then have the momentum to move toward behaviors—not because we are trying to earn anything, but because we are *becoming* something. If an individual uses this model as an excuse to not worry about personal behaviors because *the gospel is just about love,* momentum will never last. However, the more love and acceptance we truly feel from God, the more desire we will have to improve our behaviors.

Many people probably feel like a behavior-focused lifestyle is working for them. Many pride themselves on how consistent their righteous behaviors are, like weekly temple attendance, daily scripture study, in-home visits to their assigned ministering families, etc. But no matter how hard or consistently they push toward the behavior side of the continuum, the power of shame and failure will at some point catch up to them. Just like the gravity of grace pulls them toward love, the gravity of shame can get them stuck in behaviors. Remember, the goal isn't to see how long we can stay on the behavior side of the continuum. Our behaviors will never be stronger than the accepting grace of Jesus Christ. He will always pull us back to His love to remind us that behaviors don't define us.

A few years ago, a good friend invited me to attend a Warrior Heart Boot Camp, a non-denominational Christian men's retreat. At first I was very resistant. I thought it was a therapy retreat for men addicted to pornography. That isn't something I struggle with, and spending three days in a cabin in the woods wasn't appealing to my modern-technology-loving heart. My friend assured me that I had the wrong impression of the retreat. It seemed innocent enough, and I agreed to attend. It only took me a few hours at the retreat to realize this approach was simple and incredibly effective. There was no therapy involved, no woo-woo meditation

55

in the woods. It was merely a retreat focused on the love of God, coupled with an invitation to ponder and journal alone throughout the day. It would be impossible for me to articulate the experience effectively here. Later, after returning home, I realized this retreat allowed God to remove me from my daily routine—a place where I was pushing toward behaviors—and helped turn me toward His pure love and acceptance.

Since my first experience at the Warrior Heart Boot Camp, I have invited hundreds of other men to attend this same retreat. I have seen lifelong Latter-day Saints, many of them serving as bishops or in stake presidencies, approach me during the retreat bewildered that they are having such a strong experience of Godly love. One stake president told me at the end of the retreat, "I had no idea how far off track I was until attending this retreat." It would be easy to assume a stake president would be the most on track. But the busy routines and list of behaviors required of Church leaders can cause them to only push themselves toward the behavior side of the continuum. All attendees returned to their traditional Latter-day Saint lives more able to re-engage in righteous behaviors with the momentum that comes from God's love.

The nature of the restored gospel doesn't need a supplemental men's retreat. We have quorums and Relief Societies that could easily offer a more heart-focused reminder of the gospel. However, our religious culture sometimes gets hyper-focused on the continuum's behavior side, and we aren't sure what else to do other than meet every other week to discuss conference talks and share behavioral-focused Sunday School answers. Of course, there is nothing wrong with studying conference talks, behaviors, or covenants. But when we try to build spiritual momentum by pushing toward behaviors, the heart suffers—we find little purpose and often disengage from the gospel when we believe it's only about qualifying for God's love through specific behaviors.

When we understand the nature of the Gospel Continuum, we can see how the assumption of a disappointed God can really hamper the fluidity and momentum of our gospel experience. If we assume God is disappointed in our behaviors, we don't feel worthy to swing back toward His love. So we get stuck trying to get the behaviors right so we can swing back. The irony in this approach is that the love of God is what gives us the momentum to swing back toward His behaviors and do better. God isn't disappointed in our failed behaviors—He simply wants to pull us back toward love. Love, not shame, is the great motivating force in His economy.

Movement Is Progress

Relating spiritual progression to a swinging pendulum can feel odd. How are we making any progress when it seems like we are simply swinging back and forth between heart and behavior? It is important to see the Gospel Continuum as we see the speedometer in a car or a heart rate monitor connected to a patient in the hospital. Even though these dials or monitors seem to be moving up and down or back and forth they still indicate progress. When there is movement or momentum on your personal Gospel Continuum that means you are progressing, improving, and repenting. It is when the momentum stops that issues arise. We need to build momentum again by allowing the gravity of grace to move us toward love, which builds momentum and then propels us toward behaviors when the time is right.

Several years went by after Gloria's emotional breakdown on her neighbor's porch. Gloria continued to try to check all the behavioral boxes and earn God's acceptance. She hoped this was the key to diminishing God's disappointment in her. Finally, the gospel's demands became so emotionally crippling that she found herself deeply depressed. She approached her husband and explained that she needed a break from the gospel (or what she had interpreted as the gospel). She dramatically let go of all the behavioral expectations she had put on herself. She didn't commit to a life of sin—she simply let go of the idea that her behaviors defined her relationship with her Father in Heaven. Though she didn't completely stop going to church or praying, she simply stopped worrying about how these actions impacted her relationship with God. Gloria let go of the behavior side of the continuum, which allowed the gravity of grace to pull her toward God's love. Over time, Gloria noticed her testimony began to grow in a new way. When she took a "break" from the gospel, she realized she was actually offering her heart to God from a new starting point. She is now a "new creature" on her way to "inherit the kingdom of God" (1 Corinthians 6:9). When I asked Gloria if she believes God is ever disappointed in her, she responded, "My answer five years ago would be 'all the time,' but now I think disappointment is a mortal way of looking at how God feels about us when we make mistakes. God plays the long game, and when we make mistakes, He sees it as part of our development and is always there to encourage and teach" (Gloria, personal communication with author).

CHAPTER 4

Identity

Our Father in Heaven explained His purpose succinctly to Moses: "For behold, this is my work and my glory—to bring to pass the immortality and eternal life of man" (Moses 1:39). Most Latter-day Saints memorize this familiar scripture, and it communicates so much hope related to God's eternal plan. Have you ever wondered what Satan's "work" is? If we were to write it down in a simple way like Moses 1:39, what would it read? Is it Satan's work to make us unhappy? To alter the plan of salvation? To make us sin? Is there one scripture we could point to that would succinctly explain the adversary's work?

What about Moses 4:3? There we learn that the work of the adversary is "to destroy the agency of man." As a young boy, I remember learning about the War in Heaven and how Lucifer attempted to be the Redeemer, proclaiming, "I will be thy son, and I will redeem all mankind, that one soul shall not be lost, and surely I will do it" (Moses 4:1). This doctrinal explanation would typically lead to my Primary teacher saying something about how Lucifer wanted to take away our agency and force us to return to our Heavenly Father. In my young mind, I often wondered how Lucifer would carry out his plan. Could he force us to keep the commandments and not sin? Would he chain us up and lead us around mortality, forcing us to walk old grandmas across the street? Would he force us to attend the temple every week at gunpoint? My young mind would eventually get distracted, and my teacher would explain that Christ was always meant to be the Redeemer from the beginning. We often think of the War in Heaven as ending when Lucifer was cast out of heaven, but the war never ended—it still carries on today. That means Satan still has the same intention from the beginning—"to destroy the agency of man." How does Satan attempt to destroy our agency, especially when it is such a core doctrine? Especially when it was given to us by God?

The adversary can't destroy our agency, but he sure can make us feel powerless to use it. He executes his work by persuading us to alter our identity; and he does this through a potent tool—shame.

"I Am"

When I was a young boy my parents told me the story about the debate they had before they named me. There were two names on the table: Kevin and Kurt. My dad wanted to name me Kevin, and my mom wanted to name me Kurt. My mom's preference prevailed. Growing up, I thought Kurt was a strange name. I rarely heard anyone else called by my same name. When I heard I could have been named Kevin, that seemed like a much cooler name. I remember asking my parents if I could change my name to Kevin. Of course, they dismissed my request and figured this idea would pass. Then one day in fourth grade, a substitute teacher showed up in our class. As she was going through the roll, I noticed a few kids had one name on the roll but would go by an abbreviated or different name in the class. So when the teacher got to my name, I said,

IS GOD DISAPPOINTED IN ME?

"My name is Kurt, but I go by Kevin." She accepted this request without hesitation, and the rest of the day I felt an extra surge of energy every time she called me Kevin.

Names are of eternal significance in the gospel. We learn about several prophets in the scriptures who received new names, including Israel (Jacob), Paul (Saul), and Adam (Michael). Names and "new names" play a significant part when we worship in the temple. Names are important to our Father in Heaven. Names project a certain identity. Names carry a specific meaning for all of us. Even though I went through a "Kevin phase," I now appreciate my name. My middle name is Harold, which was my great-grandfather's first name. Since I was so sensitive to my first name as a child, you can imagine how much I hated telling people my middle name. I thought Harold sounded like an old grandpa's name. But now I also love my middle name because it speaks of my heritage. It reminds me of my great-grandfather and the wonderful man he was, which encourages me to be a better man.

Jesus Christ has several names and titles: Jehovah, the Savior, the Christ, etc. The name of the Savior I love the most is "the Great I Am" (Doctrine and Covenants 29:1). What a mighty name! It feels so godlike. "And God said unto Moses, I Am That I Am: and he said, Thus shalt thou say unto the children of Israel, I Am hath sent me unto you" (Exodus 3:14). Every time we say "I am," which is multiple times a day, we should see it as a moment when we reveal the Godlike nature within us. Whatever follows those two simple words is preceded by power. "I am" will act like rocket fuel to whatever words follow.

"I am" is a statement of identity. In a simple phrase, it tells us where we come from and describes the power within us. That is the power of identity—it not only defines us by name but has the power to influence our mindsets, moods, goals, and even abilities. In the book *The Alter Ego Effect* Todd Herman explains how all-star athletes like Bo Jackson and Kobe Bryant relied on an alter ego, an ideal identity, to perform at their highest level. As Bo Jackson was developing as a young player, he was inconsistent and overly emotional, which would sometimes lead to uncontrollable rage on the football field. Over time, Jackson found the powerful identity he wanted to manifest on the field. Once he found it, every time he stepped on the field, he became a new person and performed excellently.

I remember experiencing similar feelings when I served as a young bishop. I was only twenty-eight years old when I started the calling, and I was terrified to carry out my leadership duties. I felt like an imposter and that people only saw me as a young boy who knew nothing about being a good bishop. However, there was something about putting on a suit with a strong tie and having people call me Bishop Francom that propelled confidence in me.

Author Stephen Covey spoke about our godlike connection to heaven:

> Every person on earth is literally God's son or daughter and therefore has infinite potential. But if we believe that we are merely God's creatures, fundamentally and unalterably different in nature and inferior to him, our sense of self-worth and our capacity to reach our divine potential will be severely restricted.

We are literally his children, spiritually begotten. In our "spirit DNA" we are one generation from Elohim, our Eternal Father.[21]

Does that thought energize you and increase your own sense of personal potential? This is the power of identity. Again, it's literally who we are and, therefore, at the foundation of how we act.

Identity is where the cunning plan of the adversary is focused. For him, focusing on behaviors is a short game, but corrupting our identity is the long game. Before any of us acts out a behavior, good or bad, we conceive a subconscious identity statement. When Stephen Covey served as a mission president, he and his wife wrote a letter to every convert who joined the Church in their mission. They did this to understand the key elements in the new convert's conversion better. Covey was shocked by what he learned from the converts' replies. "One theme recurred over and over in all of those letters. It was this: They never really doubted the Church and the gospel, but they often doubted themselves."[22] The adversary focused on their identity to destroy their agency.

The Tool of Identity

In Moses 4 we read the story of when the serpent, Lucifer, approaches Eve to tempt her to eat the forbidden fruit. It is easy to see this exchange as being all about the behavior of eating the forbidden fruit; however, Lucifer quickly makes it more about identity: "For God doth know that in the day ye eat thereof, then your eyes shall be opened, and ye shall be as gods, knowing good and evil" (Moses 4:11).

Lucifer led out with the selling point of identity: *If you eat this fruit, you will become something more; you will identify yourself with the gods.*

In Matthew 4 we learn of the Savior fasting forty days and forty nights. The devil begins to tempt him: "If thou be the Son of God, command that these stones be made bread . . . If thou be the Son of God, cast thyself down [from the pinnacle of the temple]" (Matthew 4:3–6). It was never about how good the bread tasted or how remarkable it would feel to fly. The devil was challenging Christ's identity because that was the source of Christ's power. Christ was the Son of God and knew His mission was to help all of God's children understand their own identities. The complete knowledge of His identity propelled His mission forward, and Satan knew that was the best point of attack. If Christ lost His identity, the foundation would crumble, and the adversary would have destroyed Christ's mission.

With this new perspective of temptation, consider how the adversary is attempting to attack your heart through identity. Can you see the power the adversary gains by convincing us that our Father in Heaven is perpetually disappointed in us? Over time this has a dramatic effect on our identity. We begin to question our place in God's plan, the love that God has for us, and whether we are indeed "worthy" of His eternal blessings. In this state of mind, our agency loses power, or it feels like it loses power, and we are more likely to give up and act out in ways that are against God's commandments.

The adversary stole this tactic from our Father in Heaven. God, too, tries to draw us to Him through identity. As I mentioned before, all throughout the scriptures He gave specific individuals a new name or identity. Through His restored gospel we have been singing songs like "I am a Child of God" since our earliest memories. In recent years, God has sent a clear message of identity through His living prophet, President Nelson. In May of 2022, during a Worldwide Devotional for Young Adults, our prophet emphasized three identities: "No identifier should displace, replace, or take priority over these three enduring designations: 'child of God,' 'child of the covenant,' and 'disciple of Jesus Christ.'"[23] God gave us this great gift of agency and knows He can't force us to behave a certain way—nor does He ever try to manipulate us through negative identity statements, as the adversary does. When the devil comes tempting, one of the most powerful things we can do is fight fire with fire.

I love the story of when Moses goes up to the mountain and speaks with God. The devil tempts Moses to worship him instead of God. How does Moses respond to this temptation? With an identity statement: "And it came to pass that Moses looked upon Satan and said: Who art thou? For behold, I am a son of God, in the similitude of his Only Begotten" (Moses 1:13).

Identity statements can be one of our most potent tools to fight off temptation, even when temptation has influenced us to act out in destructive behavior. If you don't know where to start to overcome the temptation, start with an identity statement.

The Shame Chain

I'm intrigued by the visual description of Moses 7:26: "And he beheld Satan; and he had a great chain in his hand, and it veiled the whole face of the earth with darkness; and he looked up and laughed, and his angels rejoiced."

One typically sees a chain as a tool of control. A chain forces objects to either stay put or to move in a specific direction. This chain, or form of control, in Moses 7 can be interpreted in many ways. It is a good representation of shame, which is one of the devil's most vital tools. As I said before, as a young Primary student, I thought that if we had gone with Lucifer's plan, he would chain us up and force us to do things to not lose our souls. Now I understand that the adversary doesn't control us through physical chains but rather metaphorical chains of shame.

It's easy to see shame in the context of sin. We have all sinned before, felt guilty, and then felt the feelings of shame that the adversary wants us to feel. But the adversary uses the shame chain in multiple aspects of life to alter our identity.

Shame and Guilt

Guilt is typically explained as feeling bad for *doing* something wrong, and shame is typically explained as believing you *are* something wrong. These standard definitions appear simple, but I'm not sure it helps us recognize shame in a way to combat it. Typically, guilt is the initial feeling we experience when we act against our values. If I'm not looking where I'm walking in the grocery store and I suddenly knock over a sweet old lady, guilt immediately overcomes my body. I would help her up, asking her if she is okay. I would then find a place for her to sit down while calling one of her adult children to come drive her home. I would then check in on her well-being during the following few days. I would feel guilt during this entire time and would want to correct the situation because causing hurt is against my values. However, what if I was knocking down two or three old ladies in the grocery store a week? I would be vulnerable because the adversary has a chance to push me past guilt into shame, which can then impact my identity.

The adversary is always looking for the opportunity to attack our identity by pushing us past guilt into shame. This is difficult to do when our negative behaviors are common missteps, innocent mistakes, or infrequent events (like knocking over grandma). I have observed three characteristics that influence shame to surface over a behavior: the behavior (1) carries many stigmas, (2) is done repeatedly, and (3) has a high level of enjoyment or payoff. Now, thankfully, I don't think anyone is consistently knocking over grandmas in the grocery store and enjoying it, but consider the behaviors that do carry a stigma, are done repeatedly, and have some level of enjoyment (pornography use, binging media, neglecting responsibilities). Suppose the adversary can get you caught in this trifecta. In that case, he is in a position to alter your perceived identity—not only did you do something bad, but he reminds you that most people don't do that (stigma), you did it many times (repetition), and you enjoyed it (payoff). This puts you in a perfect place to be pushed past guilt into shame and for your perceived identity to be altered, which leads to more bad behavior.

It's obvious how this shame trifecta is involved in addictions like pornography or substance abuse. There's a massive stigma around these behaviors, they are repeated often, and they give a considerable level of enjoyment. Those struggling with addiction become buried in shame and are vulnerable to identity alteration by the adversary. They feel trapped. However, this shame trifecta tactic also works against all of us in our daily lives.

Imagine you are a busy mother doing your best to raise wonderful children. You find yourself hyper-focused on some social media clips related to an "influencer" you enjoy following. You lose track of time until your six-year-old reminds you that she is starving. You notice it is almost 3 p.m. and you still haven't fed your children lunch. You immediately feel guilt, but then the adversary wants to move you past guilt into shame so that he can alter your perceived identity. You will then think about how your behavior as a mom is atypical, since most parents feed their children on time (stigma), this is one of many parental slipups you have had that week (repetition), and you realize you enjoy your social media time too much (payoff). You suddenly fall into the shame trifecta. You begin to believe you are a negligent mother and that God must be disappointed in who you are (identity).

Once you recognize the shame trifecta, you can help yourself and others avoid it. For example, when my wife and I got married, we talked about having a large family—maybe even as many as seven kids. As we began trying to start a family, we were disappointed time and time again. For years we struggled with infertility until my wife finally became pregnant. The disappointment increased when that pregnancy and several consecutive pregnancies ended in miscarriage. After five years of heartbreak, we wondered if even one child was in our future. Finally, a baby girl blessed our life. She was definitely worth the wait, and we cherish our relationship with her. We were encouraged by the chance to have a larger family when my wife became pregnant a few years later. Thankfully, no miscarriage stopped the baby's growth, and we soon welcomed our first little boy to the family. However, within the first few days of his life, we noticed something was wrong. He was diagnosed with Hirschsprung's disease, which requires surgery but is entirely curable. The doctors assured us that this congenital disability was a random act of nature and had nothing to do with any diet or behavioral choices my wife had made during pregnancy. Our little boy was in the hospital for almost a month, and each day felt like an eternity. I could see how much this stress weighed on my wife, but it was a unifying trial for our family. Even though our dream of having seven kids seemed like a distant miracle, we moved forward with hope to grow our family. Little did we realize how much more heartache and loss lay ahead. Over the next few years, we experienced several more miscarriages and a traumatic ectopic pregnancy that required emergency surgery.

A few months after the ectopic pregnancy, my wife and I were chatting together, considering the possibility of trying once again to grow our family. It was refreshing to see my wife still encouraged by the possibility even though we had been heartbroken so many times. My wife wanted to give us the best chance of having another child, and she said, "Before we start trying to get pregnant, let me take a month or two and focus on my diet. Maybe if I remove all processed foods and sugars from my diet, this will give us a better chance of having a healthy baby in the end." I knew that this was something my wife had been trying to do for months. In her mind, she just needed to get the behaviors right by controlling her diet to ensure the safe arrival of a healthy baby—one that went to full term and avoided prolonged hospital stays. As her husband, I could see the attack the adversary was taking against my sweet wife as she was falling into behavioral management in order to force an outcome. Of course, there's nothing wrong with behaving in a way that gives your future child the best chance at health, but I could sense that the adversary was trying to convince her that this was her fault because of who she was and how she behaved. It had nothing to do with error, but it had everything to do with identity. Below was my wife's basic thought process:

- I'm inspired to live as healthy as I can so that my next pregnancy will succeed.

- I'm going to exercise and maintain a clean diet.

- Oh, no! I overate junk food and didn't make it to the gym.

- It's been a week since I was consistent with my exercise and diet.

- I can't seem to get into a healthy spot, and now it is more likely I won't have a healthy baby.

- There's something wrong with me.

The adversary took my wife's experience with infertility and mixed it with the shame trifecta: "Most people have babies without issue" (stigma), "I keep eating unhealthy" (repetition), and, "The food tastes so good it is hard to avoid it" (payoff). She landed on an identity statement of, "I am broken." Recognizing this crooked path to identity, I stopped my wife and reminded her that even though a healthy diet and increased exercise could encourage a healthy pregnancy, whenever that baby arrived in our family, it would be one-hundred-percent a miracle from God. Her nutritional choices had nothing to do with her identity. She wasn't broken.

I'm happy to report that my wife did become pregnant again, and we welcomed another sweet daughter into our family. My wife's identity is set with her Father in Heaven. He isn't disappointed when she doesn't skip dessert or fails to exercise. He knows her journey will include many healthy days but never feels disappointed on the bad days.

Earning Identity Through Behaviors

It's crucial to be constantly aware of the shame trifecta. Once we recognize it we must turn toward a positive identity statement to help us reset (like Moses did), remove thoughts of Godly disappointment, and carry on. When the adversary breaks down our identity through the shame trifecta, we naturally embrace this perceived identity. Of course, we don't want to believe it, so instead of stating and reminding ourselves of our divine identity, we respond with behaviors in order to reject the perceived identity— more and more behaviors. We set a new, ambitious goal and swear that this time will be different. This time we will show the world that we aren't broken. This time pornography won't be the drug of choice. This week I won't yell at my kids. This month I'll double my temple attendance. Our increased behavioral efforts often lead to improvement. We white-knuckle through behaviors and see some consistency build, and now the shame is at arm's length. Through our behaviors, we feel like we are getting ahold of our identity. In reality, our success is a failure in disguise. We ran the entire race backward. We are running toward proving our identity by crossing the finishing line when we already had it at the starting line. Suddenly we trip and fall back into old habits. Because we never embraced our true divine identity initially, and because our behavior-driven attempts to improve don't seem to succeed, we begin to believe the broken identity perception the adversary is offering us. It is easier to give up and move toward more negative behaviors because it feels like our broken identity is set.

We try to bury our shame by overcompensating behaviors that seem distant from our broken identity. Or we have no idea how to alter our identity, so we feel like the only thing to do is stay on the behavioral side of the continuum. Maybe we feel shame about how we treat our family at home, so we overcompensate by behaving like a "nice guy" at the office or at church. Maybe each night you numb out with pornography, so you spend the rest of the day breaking

KURT FRANCOM

sales records at your job. We kid ourselves by thinking that some level of behavior success on *some* plane will then set the stage to fix our broken identity or hide it. More money will make more therapy available. A higher level of scripture study will change you into the father you are supposed to be. We fail to swing to the heart of divine identity on the continuum and instead get stuck pursuing behaviors. As Stephen Covey taught, "Only when [we] have a deep conviction of [our] real identity . . . can [we] feel the inner security to turn to the Lord and align [our] souls with the Atonement."[24]

The Hook of Perceived Identity

Throughout his service as a General Authority and as President of the Church, Thomas S. Monson shared countless stories of his time serving as a young bishop of the Sixth-Seventh Ward. When I served as a bishop, these stories would often inspire me to be more caring and seek after specific individuals in need of connection and service. However, sometimes these remarkable stories reminded me of how much I was not measuring up.

I remember one instance there was an older gentleman in my ward who was suffering from cancer. One weekend he was admitted into the hospital for intensive treatment. I was so overwhelmed and distracted on Sunday that when Monday arrived, I had forgotten that this good brother was in the hospital. Suddenly, it was Thursday, and I realized I hadn't even attempted to reach out to him as he lay lonely in the hospital. If Bishop Monson was in charge of my ward, he probably would have spent the entire weekend at the hospital holding this man's hand and reading scriptures to him. But Bishop Francom was in charge, and I completely dropped the ball. I was failing as bishop and, even worse, I was sort of a lousy human. What

IS GOD DISAPPOINTED IN ME?

type of person completely forgets that a friend is in the hospital suffering from cancer? Do you recognize the shame trifecta in this scenario? Bishop Monson (and probably most bishops) don't make this error (stigma). This instance reminded me of so many other times I dropped the leadership ball (repeat) because I was more focused on myself than on others (payoff).

As I shared this experience with other experienced leaders, they all had similar situations where their actions or lack thereof made them identify as poor leaders. I'm willing to bet that Bishop Monson had days he dropped the leadership ball as well, but it's interesting how our brain rarely remembers those.

We're all susceptible to the trap of measuring our identities with behavioral measuring sticks. This cycle becomes even worse when we use someone else's behavioral measuring stick (like Bishop Monson's) to measure our own worth and identity. The adversary prods us with these measuring sticks to get us trapped in shame and then hooked by a false identity.

Being hooked by perceived identity is so common that there is an abundance of research on the topic in the therapeutic world. One popular modality that addresses perceived identity is called acceptance and commitment therapy (ACT). One concept in this modality is called the *relationship frame theory*. This theory recognizes the premise that our brains are wired to help us avoid danger and negative experiences in life, continuously defining how situations are related to us and how to protect us from risk. This natural process helps us orient ourselves; but the adversary can use this process to hijack our thinking process and access our perceived identity.

For instance, as a bishop, the minute I fell into the shame trifecta I was hooked by other identities around me, like the Bishop

Monson identity. This experience with the ward member in the hospital became an opportunity for me to recognize the hook and accept that I am not Bishop Monson and was never intended to be Bishop Monson. I've come to accept that I have limitations and weaknesses, but they have nothing to do with my divine identity.

Another way you might see the relational frame theory surface in your life is when your brain tries to connect spiritual dots that aren't there. For example, let's say you are suddenly laid off from your job. You are devastated, and in your attempt to think of what you could have done differently to protect yourself from this risk, your brain (with the help of the adversary) starts creating thoughts like, *I haven't read my scriptures as diligently as I have in the past; I probably lost my job because I am not doing my part in living the gospel.* These thoughts are not helpful and are not true.

But if we accept our weaknesses and limitations, don't we stagnate? Or, if we accept that God is never disappointed in us, won't that cause us to stop trying to be better? Russ Harris, an expert on the ACT modality, says in his book *The Confidence Gap*, "Self-acceptance does *not* mean that we pay no attention to the way we behave and the impact of our actions; it simply means we let go of blanket self-judgments. Why would we do this? Because judging ourselves does not help us in any way; it does not work to make our life richer and fuller."[25] Once we accept our mortal status and recognize the adversary's tactics, we can then accept our divine identity given to us by God. Once we pair that divine identity with the overwhelming love God has for us, we find the force to swing toward God's love more fully and progress toward Him more efficiently, without barriers of shame. Again, this swing to the love side of the continuum then creates momentum to swing back toward covenants and

IS GOD DISAPPOINTED IN ME?

behaviors—which help us overcome our mortality and be better aligned with our divine identity. When we assume that God is disappointed in us, we make a self-judgment. Getting stuck trying to figure out God's perception of us (which is already set) does not help us stay fluid on the Gospel Continuum and progressing in our journey to becoming more like He is.

Avoiding the Hook of Self-Judgment

We would all benefit from working on heightening our awareness of identity hooks, or those moments of comparison within our various identities. In *The Confidence Gap,* Harris discusses tactics we can use to avoid the self-judgment thoughts our brains produce. We might do something wrong or have a bad day, and then to orient ourselves, our brain produces identity thoughts such as, *I am not very righteous; other people in my ward don't have this problem;* or *God is disappointed in me.* To "unhook" ourselves from these unhelpful self-judgments, we need to separate our identity from them. Harris suggests we use the simple phrase "I'm having a thought that . . ." before those negative thoughts. "I'm having a thought that I am not very righteous"; "I'm having a thought that other people in my ward don't have this problem." This thought process then allows us to create distance between the thought and our identity. One way I make this tactic even more useful is by altering the phrase to say, "I notice Satan wants me to have the thought that . . ." This sounds more dramatic, but it is often true. Satan is trying to pacify us into the shame trifecta with these simple thoughts. Whenever you make a mistake or have a bad day, instead of immediately thinking God must be disappointed in you, unhook yourself from that shame by stating, "I'm noticing that Satan wants me to have the thought that God is disappointed in me."

As I mentioned before, it is common to address shame through behaviors, which simply stokes the shame, making it worse. We perpetuate this trap when we try to encourage a loved one stuck in the shame trifecta. Maybe someone you care about is experiencing significant doubt in their faith. They feel like they are being judged by others for having weak faith (stigma); they can't help but question everything again and again (repetition); they are intrigued by more and more skeptical questions related to the gospel (payoff). Thankfully, they trust you and are willing to share with you their concerns. Naturally, you encourage them through behaviors by telling them to be more prayerful, only read approved Church sources, and avoid anything negative about the Church. They might try these behaviors and only feel more consumed by shame, which will drive them deeper into negative behavior. *I keep trying to pray and read the scriptures, and it isn't working, so I'll just give up; it must all be a fraud.*

Sam Tielemans, a marriage and family therapist in Las Vegas, Nevada, teaches a simple trick to determine if shame has trapped someone and misconstrued their identity. Whenever someone approaches you with a life struggle, listen to them and try to empathize with their situation. Then ask them this simple question: "What does all this say about you as a person?" If they respond with an identity statement, "I'm just not a healthy person," or, "I am just not the type of person who can trust and believe in the gospel," or, "I'm an awful person," then you know they are trapped in shame. If it is not related to identity, then you can be assured they are probably already making progress to overcome their problem. They may respond instead with something like, "I'm not sure what the problem is, but I'll figure it out," or, "I just need to plan my day more effectively the night before so that I don't run into this problem." These types of statements are encouraging because they have nothing to do with identity.

Our Identity Like God's Identity

To progress in life, we must seek to align our identity with that of our Heavenly Father. Christ taught this identity principle in Matthew 5 when he said, "Be ye therefore perfect, even as your Father which is in heaven is perfect" (Matthew 5:48). In these verses, the Savior expressed His love for our current identity while also teaching us how to take that identity to the same level as that of our Father in Heaven. We mistakenly assume God is establishing an expectation that we become perfect sooner than later. We've talked about this in previous chapters and learned that God accepts that we will make mistakes, and we should accept that same reality. Acceptance is important because acceptance is only the beginning of our road to a higher identity. If we don't first accept that we are weak, mortal, and inconsistent, we can never learn how to overcome those limitations. We must realize that God accepts that too; He accepts us exactly as we are. There's no disappointment in that acceptance. Once you have discovered what you currently are, He will show you your potential identity—your perfect identity.

Having a goal to reach perfection is not helpful. As world-renowned shame researcher Brené Brown said, "I've learned that wherever perfectionism is driving us, shame is riding shotgun."[26] It's not our job to be driven by perfectionism. It is completely the job of Jesus to make us perfect. Leave it in His hands. God is trying to help us accept our current identity so that His Son can do the work to establish our potential identity. The adversary wants us to accept our current identity so he can remind us of how far off we are from our potential identity. Satan is continually showing us evidence through our history of behavior that we are not perfect and probably won't ever be perfect. This narrative is full of shame and is nowhere near the truth.

God has given us countless behaviors (commandments and counsel) we can use to exercise sanctification and become more like Him. The problem arises when our culture (through Satan's encouragement) regularly beats us with these same behaviors. Some of these behaviors include:

- Minister to others (especially those on your assigned list)
- Attend the temple
- Magnify your calling
- Read the scriptures daily
- Share the gospel
- Facilitate the *Come, Follow Me* program in your home
- Get an education
- Be self-sufficient
- Attend to your marriage
- Keep yourself healthy as prescribed in the Word of Wisdom

These commandments and counsel don't exist as a list of things to remind us of our shortcomings; rather, they are giving us a heavenly practice field. "[Ideal behaviors] are stars to steer by: they are not a stick to beat ourselves with."[27] These ideal behaviors often get bundled together as a way to measure our "worthiness." We have beat ourselves with this term for so long that we forget the sanctifying nature of this process. Sure, some might find themselves in a place where they are "unworthy" of a temple recommend or ordinances, which is an identity statement. But how does the adversary want you to define yourself by the word "unworthy," and how does the Lord define you?

God Leads Through Identity

There are several examples of God leading us along through identity. Christ's ministry started with identity when He was pronounced "Beloved" from the heavens after His baptism. My friend, David Butler, teaches that the first word of the Restoration was all about identity—"Joseph!" God has asked us to pronounce a name and a blessing soon after a child is born. Why do we do this? To establish an identity (through the name) and bring meaning to that identity (through a blessing). The first song many Latter-day Saints sing to their children is all about identity—"I Am a Child of God." A few years later, when that same child walks into the baptismal font, what do they receive? A new identity, in the name of the Father, and of the Son, and the Holy Ghost. Almost all ordinances start with the statement of a name or identity. We go to the temple and receive a "new name." Identity. Identity. Identity. It would seem that our Father in Heaven wants us to remember who we are and Whose we are. He sees the battle for identity and the power it has to remove agency. Just like Moses did, I hope when the adversary is attacking our identity, we will respond with a strong eternal identity statement—"I am a [child] of God!" (Moses 1:13)

When Clint Pulver was a young elementary student he struggled in a particular way. He had a hard time sitting still. He was a fidgety little boy who seemed always to have a rhythm going in his feet, legs, hands, or arms. It was very distracting for his teachers and other students in his class. These tapping and fidgeting behaviors quickly became the focus of his school experience. This behavior identified him as a "problem" or as "the disruptive kid" to those around him. It became the main focus of most of young Clint's interactions with others. His principal even encouraged him to stop the behavior by sitting on his hands whenever he began to tap. Then entered Mr. Jensen, one of Clint's teachers. After a day of much tapping, Mr. Jensen asked Clint to stay after class. Clint was full of fear and assumed this was the end of his schooling days. Mr. Jensen assured him he was not in trouble. He then asked Clint, "Have you ever thought about playing the drums?" Mr. Jensen pulled out a set of drumsticks from the top drawer of his desk. Handing the drumsticks to him, Mr. Jensen said, "Hey, Clint, you're not a problem; I think you're a drummer."[28] This decisive identity moment launched Clint into a career in drumming, where he has now performed in front of tens of thousands of individuals, motivating others through his talent.[29]

This story is an excellent example of how we can battle for someone's heart rather than for their behaviors. We all probably have loved ones in our lives who are behaving in a way that we don't approve of or in a way that will lead to unhappiness. Because of this, we may be tempted to focus on their negative behaviors in an effort to change them. The best thing we can do is remind them of their identity and allow them to have a change of heart through the grace of God.

CHAPTER 5

Hold On to Commandments

When connected to a God-given commandment, behaviors are crucial to our development and play an essential role in our becoming more like our Heavenly Father. We could never truly become like Him if we simply dismissed all unrighteous behaviors. Problems arise, though, when we misinterpret the role of commandments.

Let's consider the phrase "keep my commandments" (John 14:15). I know I love God, so I should keep His commandments. But why does He use the word "keep"? We assume that "keep" is synonymous with "obey," but who, in this modern world, uses the word "keep" rather than "obey"?

"Be careful on the road and keep all the traffic laws."

"Respect your mother and keep her rules!"

We understand these sentences, but I doubt we would structure our modern speech in this way. So, is "keep" just old Bible speak for "obey," or is there a deeper meaning?

As I mentioned in previous chapters, the emphasis on behaviors, commandments, and covenants can lead to the adversary trying to define our identity through the power of shame. This becomes an easier task when behaviors not only prove that we are not righteous but also prove we don't love God (or so we think). This leads to more shame and a more negative identity.

The Greek translation of *keep* is "to guard, hold; watch over, observe."[30] The literal Spanish translation of "to keep" is "to guard." With this new perspective on the word *keep*, how different does that scripture feel when you insert these other synonyms?

If ye love me, [seek after] my commandments.

If ye love me, [guard] my commandments.

If ye love me, [desire] my commandments.

If ye love me, [hold on to] my commandments.

Consider the dramatic change these words bring to this scripture and how they remove any perceived shame or expectation of perfection.

True Purpose of Commandments

With so many commandments, we can easily assume God placed us in a challenging obstacle course called mortality where only our outward performance is measured. We trip and fall on this course and feel shame because we think we shouldn't have messed up. This obstacle-course perspective is not helpful, though, because God never gave us commandments to measure our worth—in fact, our performance doesn't influence our worth at all. I think a better analogy would be the story of a father and a son as it is told in the movie *The Heart of Man*.[31]

IS GOD DISAPPOINTED IN ME?

There once was a father who lived many centuries ago in a small village. He had one son, and they had a deep love for one another; however, the father wanted to build upon their relationship. One day he decided to make his son a violin because the father himself loved playing his own violin and wanted to teach and share this passion with his son. The father began hand-carving a beautiful violin to give to his son. Immense amounts of love and attention were put into every detail of this violin until it was complete. After months of dedicated work, the father lovingly presented the completed violin to his son. He softly showed him how to hold the violin and where to put his fingers on the strings. The father then pulled out his own violin and modeled to his son how to slide the bow across the strings in order to make beautiful music. Day after day, they practiced together, and before long, they began playing incredible duets, which deepened their love for one another.

This parable more accurately illustrates the relationship we have with our Father in Heaven. I love seeing commandments and covenants as a violin that God has placed in our hands in order to help us practice. These violin commandments allow us to turn back to Him every time we struggle in mortality. Never were they meant to be a checklist of worth. It's a beautiful model full of love and encouragement. Commandments and covenants bring us closer to our Father in Heaven and bind us to Him through actively practicing these commandments. He doesn't stand to the side, criticizing our every mistake, shaking His head in disappointment when we can't play the commandment violin very well. Instead, He picks up His violin and shows us how to play or how to *keep* or *hold on to* His commandments.

Later in this father/son parable, the son is tempted by a far-off evil desire. The son is captivated by this temptation and stops playing his violin. In his sinful trance, as he leaves his father and his violin behind, the father never abandons his own violin; nor does he attempt to physically restrain his son from moving toward sin. Instead, the father plays his violin more intensely, trying to reach his wayward son through that symbol of love and connection. Our Father is doing the same—He wants to reach us through His commandments and covenants.

When we fall into temptation or trial, the commandment violin seems impossible to play. But we were never asked to play the commandment violin perfectly; we were only asked to "hold on to" or "keep" the violin and not discard it, as we learned before. On the hard days when the devil has broken our hearts, we often tell ourselves that we aren't the violin-playing type or that we can't live up to all these commandments. When we just can't seem to get anything right and abandon certain commandments, we shouldn't assume God has given up on us and avoid returning to those commandments. We must hold on to them and, when we are ready, approach the Lord, knowing He will start with our hearts by reminding us of His love. We can ask for His help as many times as we need to as we attempt to play the commandment violin. This process has the power to heal our hearts and remind us of our identity.

It can be difficult to reconcile the unconditional nature of God's love and the high standard of commandments. When we break a commandment, it often breaks our hearts. The adversary sees it as an opportunity to redefine our identity, and we wonder if we should just give up and not deal with this "disappointed God." We can also fall into assuming the opposite extreme, believing "God is just love," and there is no need to worry about religious rules that seem impossible to obey. President Dallin H. Oaks said, "The love of God does not supersede His laws and His commandments, and the effect of

God's laws and commandments does not diminish the purpose and effect of His love."[32] Love and commandments can be reconciled. There is no battle between love and laws. They work together to offer the healing of our hearts while we *practice* commandments. By keeping these laws and commandments, we can feel an increase of love from our Father in Heaven—not because we have suddenly become worthy of His love but because by practicing these commandments we are more able to feel His love.

This is another reason a God of grace can't be disappointed. If He is disappointed when we break laws, His love can never reach us. He doesn't stop playing the violin when we stop playing ours; instead, He plays it more intensely, knowing the music that comes from His commandments will remind us of His love. When we break a law, we assume God is holding back love. In reality, He pours on even more love to strengthen us and to help us overcome our weakness. Love doesn't supersede the laws, but the effects of His love give us the strength to keep the law. When we remember how much God loves us, we will want to do nothing more than "hold on to" His commandments.

"As Long As It Takes"

Steve grew up in a Latter-day Saint home. He appreciated the gospel from a young age, excelled in sports, and loved his social life. As a teenager, he always strived to be a good young man but found himself falling into the temptation of pornography, masturbation, and promiscuity with girls. To hide this sinful identity, Steve overcompensated with a "nice guy" identity to appear like he had his life together. He made, what he calls, a ¾ repentance before his mission, telling his bishop just enough to feel "repentant enough" to keep up with the social and cultural expectations of serving a mission. Steve served a mission and found spiritual encouragement that gave him hope that he would maintain his straight-and-narrow journey after his mission. A few months after his mission, Steve fell back into his double life and then took it further into the darkness. While maintaining a near-perfect identity to his family, friends, and fellow temple workers, Steve led a dangerous double life, stealing money from his father's business to support a hidden lifestyle paying for pornography and prostitution. You might hear about Steve's actions and identify him as evil on every level, just like the adversary was trying to do. You might wonder how an individual could be so out of control that he would risk so much, lie for so long, and break sacred covenants. After courting a beautiful young lady, marrying her in the temple, and welcoming a young daughter into their family, Steve had, what he calls, *a grace moment*. One weekend when his wife was out of town, Steve had planned a long sexual bender that would feed his addiction once again. Just before he left his home to drive toward further sin, sitting in stillness, he felt consumed by God's love. God gave Steve the grace to sit with his double life and contemplate the destruction he was doing to his soul and to his family. Steve knew the truth of his double life would eventually come out. Steve knew he couldn't go on forever without being caught. Through the grace of God, his Father in Heaven reminded him of the covenant violin music. It played so loud that Steve could no longer ignore the love coming to his broken heart. He committed to change.

When Kayla, Steve's wife, returned to town, he picked her up from the airport. Kayla knew something was not right when Steve didn't take the usual way home. Steve informed Kayla they were driving to his therapist's office because his therapist could help him communicate what he needed to tell her. With the professional

IS GOD DISAPPOINTED IN ME?

therapist present, Steve began to reveal the double life he was living since long before their marriage. Kayla was beyond mad; Steve was numb. Kayla promised Steve he would never see their daughter again and left the office in a rage. Everything Steve was afraid of was happening. After several weeks, the emotion of the situation subsided enough for Steve and Kayla to begin talking again. Hurt was still present, but they began the long road to piecing their relationship together again.

Steve received restrictions on his Church membership from his bishopric and began the journey of repentance. After much time, much repentance, and even more therapy, Steve and Kayla found trust and consistency in their relationship. They found deeper healing in their marriage, and things seemed to be better forever. Unfortunately, intense therapy and repentance did not remove Steve from the reach of the adversary. Even with the support of professionals and other individuals recovering from addiction, Steve found himself once again relapsing into the darkest corners of his past. This time his relapse led to the complete removal of his Church membership. Steve assumed these dramatic consequences would motivate him enough to never be tempted again; it only took a handful of months before Steve relapsed into addiction yet again. Thinking this would be the end of any happiness, he was shocked to see Kayla not give up on him or their marriage. Even with Kayla's support, he was sure that God was tired of his stumbling and must be incredibly disappointed in him. But he was wrong.

God spoke to him. The message came in a different tone than he expected—one full of love. He felt eternal encouragement fill his heart as he heard the words in his mind, "Steve, we can do this as many times as it takes." The fact that Steve had a God in his corner that was never disappointed in him invigorated him to keep going.

Keep trying. Every morning, Steve had to commit to symbolically picking up the covenant violin by feeling God's full acceptance of him regardless of how many times he had to repent. He could at least continue to "hold on to" God's commandments and covenants. Steve's rebaptism day happened, temple blessings were restored, his marriage continues stronger than ever, and his desire to connect his heart with God's heart grows each day.

A Divine Partnership

Like Steve, we all go through struggles with commandments and covenants (even if not to that extent). We easily slip into the perspective that commandments and covenants are part of the obstacle course of mortality, and even though we know we can repent when we slip up, we assume the goal is the finish line. Little by little, God reveals that it is not about the finish line; it is always about the relationship. Christ crossed the finish line for all of us so that we can focus on our relationship with God. When we stop seeing righteousness as a title or standard that one accomplishes and more like a relationship journey, it unlocks a deeper understanding of grace.

One simplified Hebrew translation of *righteousness* has been framed as "right relationship."[33] An insightful activity I recommend is to go to the Topical Guide in your scriptures and look up the word *righteousness*. Pick out a handful of scriptures and look them up. Now, every place you read "righteousness," replace it with the words "right relationship."

- He will judge the world in the "right relationship" (Act 17:31).

- Might grace reign through the "right relationship" (Romans 5:21).

IS GOD DISAPPOINTED IN ME?

- Awake to "the right relationship," and sin not (1 Cor. 15:34).

- Nourish them with things pertaining to "right relationships" (Mosiah 23:18).

Here are a few of my favorites:

- "And the Lord called his people Zion, because they were of one heart and one mind, and dwelt in 'right relationships'; and there was no poor among them" (Moses 7:18).

- "And 'right relationships' will I send down out of heaven; and truth will I send forth out of the earth, to bear testimony of mine Only Begotten . . . and 'right relationships' and truth will I cause to sweep the earth as with a flood" (Moses 7:62).

When we see commandments and covenants as an invitation into a relationship with God, it feels more welcoming and connected to the heart.

Stephen Covey said, "We will not become perfect like Christ in this life, but we can become perfect in Christ by entering into the holy covenant, the divine partnership, that he offers us."[34] The divine partnership is righteousness. Imagine if God explained to us before we came to this mortal journey that He would be our divine partner. No matter how hard it would get, He would be right by our side, and the more covenants and commandments He gave us, the more opportunity we would have to draw on His love and help. This type of relationship is what Steve discovered in his journey; God was never disappointed in him. God was constantly by his side, reminding him that they could try to do this relationship or

KURT FRANCOM

this divine partnership as many times as it took. Elder Neal A. Maxwell said, "Repentance requires both turning away from evil and turning to God."[35] So many times we turn away from sin but fail to turn toward God and Jesus Christ because we assume They are so disappointed in us. We assume They expect us to start behaving in a certain way before we can fully turn toward Them. We assume They want out of the partnership until we climb out of the pit by ourselves. Together with God and Jesus Christ, we will overcome all through the divine partnership—not because the commandments are so difficult but because they bring us closer together. It's about the relationship, not the rules.

Give Me More Commandments

This mindset shift of seeing commandments and covenants as more about my relationship with God has deeply enriched my life. I no longer see God as a drill sergeant pointing me toward an impossible obstacle course. I never assume He is disappointed when I mess up; rather, He is my loving Father, who wants to connect and have a relationship with me. Are commandments hard to keep at times? Yes. Are there some commandments that seem silly or "not a big deal"? Yes. Some might see our strict rules against tobacco, coffee, and tea and wonder, *What's the big deal if you have a cappuccino every once in a while? Is Jesus going to keep me out of heaven because I drink coffee?* What we can miss is the opportunity in all these commandments—the opportunity to recognize natural feelings that are difficult to control. Sure, it would be easy to give in to them, but it is so much more enlightening to turn toward God and seek His partnership in overcoming our natural man. No matter how strange the commandments, I always want to keep them. When I don't keep the commandments, like Nephi, "my heart groaneth because of my

IS GOD DISAPPOINTED IN ME?

sins" (2 Nephi 4:19). I see each commandment as an opportunity to have a deeper relationship with my Eternal Father.

My Eternal God has handed me a violin to strengthen our relationship. We keep practicing, and I keep messing up. He takes a moment to point out the techniques I need to work on, offers me some bread and water to cleanse me, and allows me to start over. Then I see progress to become more like Him.

We might hear sacrament meeting talks that harp on behaviors, behaviors, behaviors. I've caught myself a time or two wondering, *Why all the behavior talk? Where's the heart?* Then I am reminded that I am in another violin lesson. When we hear lessons and talks about improving behaviors, we are simply spending some time on the behavior side of the continuum, seeking a deeper relationship with God through these behaviors. "If we accept [Jesus Christ] as our mentor, we have a relationship with him, and he enables us to have a relationship with our Heavenly Father. How can we do that? By entering into His covenant and constantly returning to it, and by looking into our hearts to see what we need to do."[36] When life gets tough and commandments seem overwhelming, turn back to God through your covenants. He's not disappointed in you; He is your Divine Partner.

CHAPTER 6

Vulnerable Wounds

Mark 9 tells the story of a father who brings his afflicted son to the Savior to be healed. What captivates me the most about this story is the father's desperation. You can almost feel it coming from the pages of the Bible. After the Savior says, "If thou canst believe, all things are possible to him that believeth," the father cries out in tears, "Lord, I believe; help thou mine unbelief" (Mark 9:23–24). As a father myself, I relate so much to this story. As I mentioned in the last chapter, when my son was born in 2015, everything seemed normal. However, more than 48 hours had passed after his birth without my son having his first bowel movement, which can be a sign of severe health issues. The doctors began running tests and, as time passed, the look in their eyes told us that something was not right. After a few hours, we found ourselves in a room with doctors and nurses carefully working on our son. As my wife and I stood by, wondering what was happening, I distinctly remember one of the doctors telling us, "Your son is very sick." At that moment, I embodied that father in Mark

9. I had no idea what was wrong with my son or how sick he was. Would he die? Would he live? Would complications follow? I was desperate for healing. I was desperate to unhook my baby from those machines and deliver him into the arms of the Savior. *Lord, I believe*, I thought. *Help thou mine unbelief.* Thankfully, our son was diagnosed with Hirschsprung's disease, a very manageable and curable disease. He went through surgery and, after twenty-five days in the hospital, came home. He is now a healthy, active young boy.

Our relationship with the Savior was never meant to be passive. He did not suffer and die so that we might have a nice eternal buddy. He suffered and died so that He could offer us eternal life and healing. Logically, we know why we need Jesus in this life and eventually at the judgment bar, but we aren't always sure why we need Him *today*. Or we understand He is our Savior, but what is He saving us from? We have to push past the abstract idea that we can't go to heaven without Jesus—which is true—to not only understand redemption in theory but to experience it in our daily lives. Anyone who has heard someone recovering from addiction talk about their daily reliance on Jesus can see how desperately they need Him each day. Jesus has become an integral part of their every day. So why can't He become that for you? Is that daily redemption only reserved for those who have fallen into addiction or have the greatest trials?

Imagine you are one of the people in 3 Nephi 17 waiting in line to receive healing from the Savior. Suddenly, it's your turn. The Savior looks at you and asks what healing you need. What would you say to Him? Would you stammer and tell Him about the cold you had last week, or ask him about your pesky sciatic nerve that keeps flaring up? Would you simply introduce yourself so that He remembers your name on judgment day? Would you be able to present to Christ a wound that causes you so much desperation, that has crippled you spiritually or emotionally to the point that you can't move on in life until you've received His healing? Or do you perceive life as merely full of manageable scratches that don't require a Savior?

Our everyday relationship with the Savior is not meant to be passive. Our repentance cannot be a superficial spiritual transaction. Elder Neil L. Andersen said, "One of the greatest stumbling blocks to receiving the divine gift of forgiveness is attempting to repent of a sin and not to repent of sinning."[37] Repenting of sinning changes our nature and brings us closer to the image of God. Moving past the sin itself and addressing the sinning requires finding our spiritual wounds and focusing on the healing required there. For example, an individual may slip up and view pornography a few nights in a row. They could then set an appointment with the bishop and go through the required steps to get it "cleared up." However, it is a whole different journey, and one that is more effective, when an individual explores the wound that caused him or her to need that moment of sinning. What hurts so much in life that causes someone to numb out through sin? Stigmatized sin isn't always the source for numbing a wound. Other coping mechanisms can include secluding from community, binging forms of media, even turning to food for comfort. Once we find that root issue, that deep wound, we then begin the true healing process. Everyone will face wounds in life that require them to turn to the Savior, desperate for healing. These wounds reveal our mortal brokenness that can only be healed by the Divine.

Even though some of us can't find immediate evidence of our own wounds, they are there, and it is necessary to seek them out because it is through those wounds that we will find a deeper relationship with Christ. The perceived feeling of godly disappointment is a good starting place to begin to find wounds in your life. If we can't determine where we are broken, it is going to be difficult to accept His redemption. Mortality broke us all in some way, and we can't simply stand at a lectern, stammer through a testimony that *Jesus lives*, and call it good. We have to point at our wounds, recognize the pain they cause, and then offer them to the Savior for healing.

Finding Our Personal Wounds

Shame and vulnerability researcher Brené Brown said, "Every single person has a story that will break your heart. And if you're paying attention, many people . . . have a story that will bring you to your knees. Nobody rides for free."[38] It's true, nobody rides for free in this life, even when life is full of abundant blessings. Nobody will return to our Father in Heaven after this life with the attitude of *Wow! That was easy.* In Philippians 2:10–11, we read the well-known passage, "That at the name of Jesus every knee should bow . . . and that every tongue should confess that Jesus Christ is Lord." We often interpret these verses to mean that someday even the wicked will have to admit that they need Christ—but these verses also apply to the righteous. Every person, including those who have been incredibly faithful in terms of behavior, will have to admit that they are deeply wounded and in desperate need of the Savior. No wound? No connection to the Savior.

We unintentionally run from Jesus when we see him as only a "rewarder" and not so much a "healer." Somehow, we misinterpret the gospel of redemption as a prosperity gospel—as if living the gospel is only about doing the behaviors right so that you are rewarded in life and avoid any hurtful wounds (remember the gospel equation in chapter 3). When life gets hard and we become wounded, we often avoid taking our wounds to God—we assume He will be disappointed in us for having wounds, for not behaving in a way that would have avoided the wounds altogether. Or we might be angry at God for inflicting us with wounds. In reality, He wants us to bring our wounds to Him because He knows they are gateways to our hearts.

There is an incredible Christian song called "Scars" by the band I Am They that perfectly articulates this dynamic of how we experience scars and wounds and how they bring us to Christ:

> *Darkest water and deepest pain*
> *I wouldn't trade it for anything*
> *'Cause my brokenness brought me to you*
> *And these wounds are a story you'll use.*[39]

I encourage you to listen to the entire song and ponder over the lyrics.

Types of Wounds

Since identifying our personal wounds is crucial to creating a doorway into our hearts for the Savior to enter, let's consider the different types of wounds individuals will encounter in life. Christian author John Eldredge has defined two categories of life wounds: assault wounds and passive wounds. Assault wounds are the most dramatic and easy to find. They are mixed with trauma and/or evil. The person who experienced sexual abuse as a child, the children of divorces, the spouses betrayed by their partners' infidelity, etc.—all these wounds are more easily recognizable. Passive wounds, on the other hand, form from the steady pressure of life, inequalities, the daily struggles to succeed—such as trying to measure up to older siblings, continuing to get cut from every sports team you try out for, or demotions at work that diminish your morale. These passive wounds can be difficult to identify. Eldredge said, "The passive wounds are . . . pernicious, like a cancer. Because they are subtle, they often go unrecognized as wounds and therefore are more difficult to heal."[40] Passive wounds appear alongside good intentions. Maybe a father was so career-focused while trying to raise his family that he was generally absent from the lives of his children. Over time, this lack of fathering could leave wounds of abandonment on the hearts of his children. These scars can impact future relationships.

Two quick words of caution when it comes to recognizing our wounds. First, it's never helpful to compare wounds. Someone who has more passive wounds might think, *Well, what do I have to complain about? I was never sexually abused as a child as others were.* It's then easy to dismiss our passive wounds because they do not seem as traumatic as others' assault wounds. It's crucial to see that all wounds, no matter how dramatic, have the power to invite Christ into our hearts. Second, we all must recognize, especially parents, that even with all the best intentions in the world, we will most likely be the cause of passive wounds in our children's lives or in the lives of other loved ones. This can generate a lot of guilt and regret. Of course, we should diligently try to avoid wounding others' hearts, but passive wounds happen either

IS GOD DISAPPOINTED IN ME?

way, simply because we are mortal. The mistakes we have made on others' hearts will be transformed into healing by the Savior and bless the lives of our children or loved ones in the long run. More on this in future chapters.

To better help you identify these wounds in your heart, let's discuss how these wounds manifest themselves. We'll start with assault wounds, followed by passive wounds.

Wounds from Others' Poor Choices (Assault)

Some individuals make poor (even sinful) choices that impact others. This includes all abuse, assaults, infidelity, and addictions. Maybe a father chooses to be unfaithful to his wife and leaves his family. His former spouse now wrestles with trusting others, and the children struggle with a sense of abandonment that lasts into adulthood. Their father's actions left a wound that the Savior must heal.

Wounds from Traumatic Experiences (Assault)

These wounds are similar to those that come from others' poor choices, but sometimes trauma happens in life regardless of whether it is related to a particular individual's actions. This would include tragic accidents, intense medical diagnoses, death, poverty, and war. Maybe the economy goes south, and you lose a job; maybe a tire blows out and causes an awful car accident; maybe you get lung cancer without ever smoking a cigarette. Good people die suddenly and unexpectedly. Sometimes couples can't seem to get pregnant when they plan to. There are so many examples of this type of wound. But, in short, life often causes painful wounds that Jesus needs to reconcile, through no fault of our own.

KURT FRANCOM

Wounds in Our Nature (Passive)

These types of wounds include sin but can also include natural trials that we may encounter in this mortal life—for instance, strong sexual attraction, mental illness, or even physical limitations and disabilities in our own life or in the lives of those we love. We have been born into a fallen world. We are children of God, but in mortality, two imperfect mortals created us. We are taught that "the natural man is an enemy to God" (Mosiah 3:19). Naturally, we are prone to be prideful and selfish. Over time, and through the mentorship of parents and society, we are encouraged to be more selfless.

This "natural man" is a wound we are born with that the Savior must reconcile. Naturally, without the guidance of eternal gospel principles, we would easily indulge in a life of sinful behavior. We are not bad people because we naturally want to sin; this is simply part of our nature of being born into a fallen world. It's a wound that we must take to the Savior for reconciliation and healing. Or naturally, individuals are born with certain physical or mental disabilities that bring hardship. Some individuals experience same-sex attraction and have to reconcile this part of their identity with God's commandments—I want to be very clear that I'm not trying to label same-sex attraction as a type of handicap; it is merely part of some individuals' natural identity that must be reconciled through the Savior.

Wounds from Others' Poor Choices (Passive)

The choices of others can cause assault wounds, but they can also cause passive wounds, even with the best intentions. This would include less-than-ideal parental relationships, divorce, or difficulties in marriage. A father consistently missing his son's little league games to try to meet deadlines and provide for his family may leave children with wounds of abandonment and disconnection. Or the wife who has no concept of how to nurture her husband when he desires deeply to return to school to change his career. No matter how many counseling or relationship courses we attend, we have to get to a place where we reconcile the wound with the Savior and find the strength to change, repent, and carry on through Him.

Wounds from Resisting the Grace of Jesus Christ (Passive)

I will discuss more related to these types of wounds in my own story in the coming pages, but this type of wound often comes from the overwhelm of life, when we get stuck on the behavior side of the Gospel Continuum. We're trying to do it all and expect near perfection. We misunderstand the gospel as a list of boxes to check to define our identity and worth to others and God. We run ourselves ragged and develop wounds that the Savior needs to reconcile.

Wounds from the Wickedness in Ourselves and in the World, Including the General Battles of Mortality (Passive)

Scriptures and modern-day prophets prophesied that the world would grow more and more wicked. We have been in a spiritual battle with the adversary since the premortal existence. These wounds include living in a world that normalizes sin and decreases religious values. These wounds also include the general friction of life, including demotions or layoffs at a job, lack of marriage opportunities for some, and general missed opportunities that cause regret and wound the heart. This even includes our poor decisions or sinning that have caused consequences that make life more difficult. The constant battle of mortality causes friction in life that creates wounds. We must turn toward the Almighty for healing.

Questions to Identify Wounds

Identifying specific wounds in life can be more difficult for some than for others. It may take several days, months, or years of pondering before we are able to find and surrender the many levels of our wounds to the Lord. Thankfully, He wants to help you and is ready to guide you on this path. Here are some questions to ponder or journal about to help uncover your wounds:

- Is there an event or topic in your past that loved ones taught you never to discuss?

- Were there specific standards in your home growing up that caused you to feel like you had to earn love through specific actions or behaviors (such as earning certain grades, performing well athletically, serving a mission, etc.)?

- Are there certain sins or habits you can't seem to stop repeating? Most (if not all) compulsive sins or addictions are linked to specific wounds (more on this in the next section).

- What moments in your life do you wish you could go back and attempt again? Why?

- Do you often feel concerned about what other people think about you?

- Do you try to control the feelings of others through your actions? (For example, being nice to try to make someone feel happy)

IS GOD DISAPPOINTED IN ME?

- Was there a significant goal in your life that never came to be?

This list of questions is not comprehensive. Sometimes it can be beneficial to meet with a professional counselor to help uncover certain wounds that may be a little too deep to heal without additional help.

When a wound forms, it shows up on the heart (symbolically)—or, in other words, wounds show up emotionally, and, therefore, we tend to bury them emotionally because of the shame they bring on. This is why the contrast between heart and behavior is so vital to understand. We think we are healing our wounds through more diligent behavior when behaviors only act as a shovel to bury wounds. Then, when we assume God is disappointed in us, we try to bury our wounds more quickly before He notices, similar to a child hiding his or her mistake under the bed before the parent walks into the room. This was the first tool Satan employed against Adam and Eve, and they hid. This burying-and-hiding process is the trap of shame. We try to forget the hidden wound, but the adversary continuously reminds us of the pain, causing us to expend more energy to better bury it instead of laying it at the feet of the Master Healer.

Discovering My Wound

This concept of seeking out and identifying my spiritual and emotional wounds seemed odd to me at first—even made me skeptical. I've never been abused, I had a wonderful childhood, and I have never experienced poverty—so why can't I just focus on the abundant blessings of my life? Seeking out my wounds sometimes feels like I am dismissing or ungrateful for the incredible blessings God has given me. I now realize this is not a binary discussion. I can feel a sense of overwhelming gratitude for blessings and still recognize where life hurts. The person who breaks an arm does not dismiss the pain simply because both her legs still work. Our gratitude for blessings connects us with God, but not to the degree of healing our wounds. God doesn't only want to bless us—He desires to have us bring our wounds to Him for healing and connection. Even though my life has been very positive, I had to do—and am still doing—the work to find those passive wounds. Ignoring the possibility of passive wounds, like avoiding the potential of hidden cancer, is not helpful. I would be missing out on potential healing, which would lead to a deeper relationship with my Father in Heaven.

My journey of seeking out the passive wounds in my life has been one of my greatest blessings. As I have spent countless hours reflecting on my life and considering where wounds might be hiding, I have felt a deeper relationship develop with my Father in Heaven and my Savior. I've uncovered memories of feeling inadequate during my education years. I quickly realized the unintentional hurt created by the circumstances of being three years younger than my brother, who excelled in schooling. Many people and organizations showered him with accolades and full-ride scholarships, while I wondered if I would ever be smart enough to measure up. I struggled to get Cs as my brother seemed to get straight As with far less effort. Of course, there is nothing wrong with my brother excelling in school, and I have no doubt he worked hard for those grades. And, of course, there is nothing wrong with my parents applauding his success (especially when they didn't have to figure out how to pay for his college). But the adversary, seeing an opportunity to identify me as the "dumb brother," began to leverage my wound. This wound continued to surface for me, even in college. I remember sitting in a college counselor's office, trying desperately to figure out how to graduate and move on with my life. When she told me what classes I would have to retake, I was brought to tears as the wound of inadequacy became inflamed again. *You're still dumb and may never finish college. You still don't have what it takes.* Those are the thoughts that screamed from my wound. I eventually graduated from college with a degree, but still, that wound of being the "stupid kid" still emerges from time to time.

Just this year, more than a decade after graduating from college, my wife and I were trying to qualify for a home loan. I have been self-employed for many years, and the process of qualifying for a loan is a lot more complicated than if I had a traditional job with a steady income. Mortgage brokers want to see consistent pay stubs as evidence that we have a consistent income. Being self-employed, there are no pay stubs, and the process became very complicated. Several mortgage lenders told us that we would not qualify for a home loan. That's when the shame of it all inflamed that same wound. Here I was, approaching forty years of age, and the adversary's message was loud and clear: *You still don't have what it takes to provide for your family. The stupid kid just can't measure up.* I'm happy to report that, through persistence and finding the right lender, we were able to qualify for the home loan, but still, despite the countless blessings in my life, the wounds still scream at times.

It has been so healing to sit with these wounds, take them to my Father in Heaven, and have Him validate my identity as His child. I could have easily ignored those wounds, buried them, and carried on with life, blaming greedy mortgage lenders or ignorant school teachers who didn't understand my brilliance and creativity. Instead, I recognized where it hurt and sought out healing from above.

Finally, I'd like to share with you one more wound I unexpectedly discovered. It was a wound I was blind to, and asking specific questions brought it to the surface for healing.

In March of 2019, I found myself struggling with some of my behaviors—or rather, lack of behaviors—that triggered a lot of shame for me. I typically work each day in my home office at my standing desk. I also have a sit-down desk on the other side of my office, and my scriptures usually sit on that desk. At that time in my life, I had work and life demands that kept me very busy (like most people), and my daily scripture study routine was out of whack. In the past, I had great success with building a routine around scripture study that seemed bulletproof, but now I couldn't seem to establish any consistency. It was almost as if my scriptures were taunting me, providing a constant reminder of my inadequacy as a good, daily-scripture-studying Latter-day Saint: *Hey, Kurt, here I am, just sitting here on this desk. You know, you should read me. Remember, good Latter-day Saints should be doing daily scripture study. I can't believe you've been a bishop before, and you still can't figure out how to read your scriptures.*

Sometimes this imaginary mockery would lead me to say, *Fine! I'll read.* I would plop down on the chair by the desk, open the scriptures, and try to read. Most of the time, I was just reading words on a page. I would read long enough for the shame to die down, and then I would return to my work, wondering what was wrong with me (an attack on my identity). Why couldn't I enjoy reading my scriptures anymore? I would recommit each day to have a more thought-out approach to my scripture study time, to be intentional and invite the Spirit. But for weeks and months, I just couldn't get any spiritual water from the scriptural well. At this point, you might default to analyzing my behaviors—maybe

IS GOD DISAPPOINTED IN ME?

I wasn't worthy; maybe I was doing something in my life that was impeding me from rich spiritual experiences during my scripture study time. What I found out later surprised me the most: it seemed that God removed any pleasure or benefit from my scripture study because He wanted to teach me at a deeper level and reveal a wound I didn't know was there.

A few months of frustrating, empty scripture study passed, and I found myself attending another Christian men's retreat in the mountains of Summit County, Utah. On the second day, before the morning session began, attendees were slowly filing into the conference lodge. I was sitting in the front row, to the side, and the conference organizers were playing some contemporary Christian music. I don't remember the specific song or lyrics, but the music offered God an opportunity to bring to my mind my scripture-study dilemma. I remember thinking, *Why can't I figure this out? Why can't I find any flow with my scripture study? I'm afraid I am disappointing God every time I don't study my scriptures.* At that moment, after offering those questions from my heart, it was as if the music went silent, and all I could hear was a clear message from my Father in Heaven. These words came to my mind: *You could never read your scriptures again, and I would still love you.* The words woke up my mind, and it was as if I didn't fully understand them until they came to my mind once more. *You could never read your scriptures again, and I would still love you.* There it was, the lesson of my journey— my wound, hiding deep under the surface.

I was stuck in behaviors, assuming that I had to earn God's love just like I had to earn so many other things in life. I was only reading my scriptures to check a box and earn some level of acceptance from God, but He wasn't disappointed when I didn't read the scriptures. His love isn't conditional on those behaviors—it is infinite. He wanted a connection with me, not because I earned it but because His grace offers it—at no cost. I had defined most of my life according to behaviors. I was obsessing over behaviors so much that God had to disrupt my system. He wanted to bring me back to the heart side of the continuum to prepare me for healing. This interaction with God helped me uncover the shame of my wound. It helped me correct these awful messages that my wound had consistently communicated. *You're not dumb. You're not falling short. You're not the stupid kid. I love you.*

I genuinely believe that in the months leading up to that conference, God took away the joy and benefit of scripture study to reconnect my heart with Him. After that moment, I'd like to say that scripture study has been more enjoyable than ever, but after returning home, I realized I was on a new journey as it relates to scripture study. Instead of routinely opening and reading the scriptures, I focus my energy on slowing down, pondering, maybe listening to spiritual music, and journaling. I focus my effort on connecting with the Divine rather than completing my scripture study. Some days, that includes more formal reading and highlighting, and other days it includes being still and listening. It has been told that Mother Teresa was once asked by an interviewer how she prayed. She responded, "I listen." The interviewer then asked, "Well, what does he say?" She answered, "He listens." I didn't have time to listen when my primary focus was checking the box.

My wound has healed by taking a more sincere listening approach to my daily devotion to God. Latter-day Saint author Carrie Skarda once taught me the power of mentally sitting by a fire with Christ. I have found this activity so enriching! I first find a quiet place before going to bed. I'll close my eyes (maybe turn on the sound of a soft campfire burning) and then envision the Savior quietly walking to the fire, sitting down next to me. Neither of us says any words. We simply sit and stare at the fire together. In these moments, I feel an overwhelm of love coming from the Savior. On the bad days, He can see the worry on my face, which leads to Him laying His arm around my shoulders, and we just sit and watch the mental fire in my mind. Scripture study and prayer are critical; for me, taking the step to first connect with the heart has become paramount. It's been a journey of discovery as the Lord has shown me more and more of His heart by removing behavioral disappointment and simply accepting me where I am at that moment. Then the healing can begin.

CHAPTER 7

Hide, Numb, or Heal

From the moment Adam and Eve partook of the fruit in the Garden of Eden, a wound formed. After eating the fruit, they discovered they were naked and felt shame for the first time in the history of mankind. Naturally, the adversary encouraged them to sew fig leaves into a covering to hide the "wound." They then ran and hid from God, as if God was the one to fear. Once God called Adam and Eve out of hiding, He introduced them to the Savior, who could heal their wound. The contrast is obvious: the adversary encourages us to hide our wounds and then hide our true nature; our loving Father encourages us to turn toward the Savior for healing. Adam and Eve were on new ground. They were not sure how to handle the consequences of their actions, so they took the adversary's advice. Shame was such a powerful experience, and they didn't know what to do with it.

Adam and Eve responded to shame much like all of us respond to shame—we hide our wounds and our true selves because we hope to maintain control of our lives. *Maybe if we hide long enough, Father will not notice that we ate of the tree, or we can fix this problem on our own. Then we can continue our lives in this beautiful garden.* Wounds can be embarrassing, have the potential to hurt others around us, and may produce scary consequences. We worry God will reject us by kicking us out of our Garden of Eden. Once we identify our wounds, we often don't know what to do with them. They hurt and can cause a lot of disruption and anxiety. We begin to feel guilt and shame because we aren't the person we want to be. We feel like our wounds are preventing us from progressing and living our best lives. We might try to ignore them, but they are too persistent and too painful. In theory, we know we need to heal wounds through the power of Christ's Atonement, but that can feel more complicated than we'd like. Just like a physical wound can lead to infection, a spiritual wound can lead to the infection of shame. When shame is present, we typically do two things: We *hide* the wound because it is embarrassing, and we *numb* the wound because it hurts.

When individuals discover wounds in their lives, it would be great if they could simply step into a closet, plead with Heavenly Father to heal that wound, receive healing, and then step out of the closet and continue with life. Nobody would know the difference. But, because wounds foster shame, they alter our perceived identities and make us unacceptable (in our minds) to other people. The adversary recognizes this shame and tells us that we are falling short of our ideal identity as righteous sons or daughters of God. It feels impossible to reconcile our wounds with our identities, so we hide—we seclude. We push everyone away from our wounds and try to heal them on our own.

Wounds often require the help of a parent, a spouse, a Church leader, or even a professional therapist to heal. If you had a broken arm, it wouldn't make sense to try to set and splint it on your

IS GOD DISAPPOINTED IN ME?

own; neither is it wise to try to work through a spiritual wound alone, especially when there may be intense trauma attached to the wound. The brain often doesn't know how to remove shame and process trauma without professional help. We might admit that we need additional help to address wounds, but we still want to maintain control. An individual might set up an appointment with his or her bishop but then request that the bishop keep this information between the two of them and quickly go through the process of "taking care of" a transgression. Or an individual might meet with a professional therapist to address anxiety but quickly ask for medications that can subdue the anxiety without addressing past trauma that is causing it.

As we try to maintain control, we battle the shame that comes with wounds. Shame is an infection on our souls, and it becomes a leverage point for the adversary to alter our perceived identities. The more he works on our identities, the more likely we are to bury wounds and never take them to the Savior for real healing. We unintentionally make one of the harshest deals with the devil—we agree to deal with the shame as long as he helps us keep the wound hidden.

We have two obvious choices when it comes to dealing with our wounds. We can either 1) hide and numb the wound to maintain control of our life. Or we can 2) take the wound to the Savior and receive healing. Reading these two options on paper might make you wonder why someone would even consider the first option. It seems so easy to take it to the Savior and receive His healing; however, when we take our wound to the Savior, it requires us to lose control of the outcome by surrendering to His will, which could lead to life getting messy. We have to be vulnerable (show our nakedness) and surrender everything to Christ. After considering that we might lose control of life, we naturally consider trying to do things on our own. We do so as a temporary measure, promising ourselves that we will, at some point, make the time and take steps to find healing through Christ. Just not today. We begin hiding and numbing wounds by posing as something we are not and/or rebelling to numb the shame pain.

Numbing Through Façades

Early in 2020, I was sitting at a stake baptism preview with a bunch of parents and their eight-year-old children. My daughter was turning eight that year and was looking forward to being baptized. As we all sat in the chapel, a member of the stake primary presidency was interacting with the children in the room who were soon to be baptized. She asked the question, "How do we keep the commandments?" Before anyone in the room could respond, one eight-year-old boy shouted, "We be nice!" Many other answers followed, but this response to "be nice" caught my attention the most.

I don't know where the concept of nice-guy syndrome first developed, but it was made more mainstream after Dr. Robert Glover published his book *No More Mr. Nice Guy* in 2003. In short, nice-guy syndrome is simply a form of co-dependency, or when individuals act in a certain way to manipulate how people act and feel around them. This might look like a child who behaves like a "good boy" to avoid the yelling of his father, or a husband who acts in a way that will increase the chances of his wife being in a good mood.

I've been living my life trying to "be nice" for years. I've been living the life of the "nice guy" for so long that I figured that was the point of living the gospel—so that we could all turn out to be

IS GOD DISAPPOINTED IN ME?

"really nice." "Being nice" is one of the most effective façades (or fig leaves) the adversary encourages us to use to cover up our ugliest wounds. I realize this might be confusing to hear. *How is "being nice" a bad thing?* Our mortal minds tend to see everything as binary, so when you read that "being nice" can be a negative thing, your mind naturally asked, *So, you think we should all be jerks?* No. The opposite of "being nice" is not "being a jerk"—it's "being real." Before I give you another example of this, it is essential to realize that even though it is referred to as nice-*guy* syndrome, it happens just the same for women as well—nice-gal syndrome is real too. Let me give you a fictional example of a man I'll call Brad.

Brad was raised in a very orthodox Latter-day Saint home. He was always taught to choose the right, to not lie, to not hit his sister, and, in general, to be a "good boy." During his teenage years, he was seen as a really "good kid," as he showed up to church each week with his hair combed, ready to bless the sacrament and give the right answers in Sunday School. In Brad's coming-of-age development, this "good boy" identity became what he thought was his true identity. He served a mission, got good grades in college, married in the temple, and his "good boy" persona quickly developed into a "nice guy" identity. This story would make any Latter-day Saint mother proud. But here is the problem.

Remember, nobody rides for free. We all have wounds in our lives that we need to take to Christ so that He can reconcile them. What I didn't tell you about Brad's story is that he never really had a strong relationship with his father. His father was so busy trying to stay ahead of the family obligations that there was no real connection between the two of them. When they did interact, it often included a lecture, reminding Brad of where he didn't measure up and about behaviors he needed to improve. As Brad discovered his sexual desires, he turned toward pornography for education because he didn't know how to ask his dad for understanding. After looking at pornography a few times as a teenager, Brad was overcome with shame and couldn't reconcile how a "good kid" like him (an identity he assumed because of shame) could have done something so terrible. Of course, he didn't want to disappoint anyone around him, so he kept his negative actions and his wound to himself. He promised to never reveal this ugly side to anyone. He would simply cover it up by being a really "good kid." As he grew older, he doubled down on the identity of being a really "nice guy." If he appeared to be a remarkable missionary, diligent student, and loyal husband, he'd never have to reveal his true self. It is reasonable why Brad would attempt to hide a wound by being super righteous, as perfect as possible, hoping the "nice guy" identity would help him bury the shame and maintain control of life.

Even if the "nice guy" façade works for a little while, every man or woman will, at some point, realize hiding the wound simply can't last. Even when we hide our wounds behind a façade, they still hurt. For some time, even years, we might find that we can deal with our hidden wounds and the shame pain that comes from them. We might even begin to assume they are healed, and we have moved past them—until a trigger in life uncovers and inflames the buried wound. In Brad's story, he reached a level of control and stability as he invested himself in his work and Church responsibilities until, one night, he and his wife got into a terrible argument. It started small, but soon their frustrations went off the charts. His wife's words hurt Brad, so he secluded himself in the basement. It was a triggering event that brought all his wounds to the surface.

IS GOD DISAPPOINTED IN ME?

The pain of the wounds was too much. Brad remembered the rejection he'd felt from his father as a child and now felt that same rejection from his wife. Soon he was online, numbing the pain through viewing pornography. This triggering event only caused the wound to grow larger.

The pornography numbing worked for that night, but then Brad had to wake up the next morning and go to work. He was drowning in shame throughout the workday because of his numbing actions from the night before. It hurt that his wife was angry at him, and he thought for sure God was disappointed in him because of the sin he'd committed. He then turned to a trusted form of numbing called "earning acceptance," and the "nice guy" knows just how to do that. He returns home after work with flowers in hand. He does what any "nice guy" would do and desperately asks his wife for forgiveness regarding their argument the night before. He takes all the responsibility for the negative interaction, and he sees her begin to smile. He cooks dinner that night and encourages his wife to take a long bath while he cleans every last dish and puts the kids to bed. By the end of the night, he feels acceptance from his wife, and it is like a soothing balm on his wounds. It feels like healing, but it is only numbing. Brad knows he needs to talk to his bishop and his wife about his choices, but he'll get to that later. He is certain God is disappointed in him, so he pleads for God's forgiveness, much as he did with his wife. Instead of giving God a bouquet of flowers, over the coming weeks Brad magnifies his calling to the nth degree. He soon receives pats on the back from his bishop and other ward council members. These accolades tell him he is truly "accepted," and it numbs his wound even further. After about a year of ignoring the memories of his sinful behavior—never opening up about it to the bishop—he assumes that it wasn't a big deal and that he's done enough repenting for that sin through his righteous behavior. He feels like progress and healing are taking place when, in reality, his shame is causing the wound to grow larger and larger, waiting for the next triggering event.

We first get introduced to the numbing power of acceptance at an early age. Like most things, it starts innocently with a parent who simply wants to raise "good boys" and "good girls." The parent praises the child with phrases like, "Great job!" or, "You are so smart!" As children, we quickly connect our behavioral performance to praise, and then we connect praise to acceptance. *The more I behave like a good girl, the more my mom hugs and loves me. When I am bad, she gets mad and sends me to my room (a feeling of personal rejection).* Of course, parents never intend for these feelings of rejection to come from their parenting styles, but, over time, that is how the child interprets it.

There is a dynamic in every human culture of praise and accolades that get misinterpreted as a form of acceptance. In our Latter-day Saint culture when we receive accolades after receiving the priesthood, serving a mission, marrying in the temple, etc., we begin to think that our behaviors are what compel others to accept us. Or—a concept connected to my personal story—when we see certain callings or titles as a form of Godly acceptance, it can be poisonous. After my brother excelled in school (which reminded me how much I was not excelling) and after he served a successful mission as a mission leader (unintentionally sending me the message that a successful mission requires the call to serve as a leader), I was committed to showing everyone in my life, including God, that I had what it took. I would be a super missionary, keeping all the rules,

IS GOD DISAPPOINTED IN ME?

achieving perfect obedience, and being a shoo-in for a leadership role. I did all that, and guess what? I never became a mission leader.

My wound of inadequacy or my wound of being the "stupid kid" became inflamed. I came home from my mission more committed to keeping the commandments as perfectly as possible. I doubled my efforts of righteousness, served as elders quorum president, married in the temple, was called as a bishop at the age of twenty-eight, and then was called to a stake presidency at age thirty-three. I assumed these callings to lead proved that I had been "successful" in the gospel. My good-intentioned, positive behaviors buried my wound until the Lord finally taught me one of my most potent lessons at that Christian men's retreat: *You could never [do a righteous thing again], and I'd still love you. You are adequate because I created you as enough.* I don't think the Lord is done teaching me that lesson, and that wound is still healing.

I am heartbroken to hear about men in their forties, fifties, and beyond who feel incredible shame because they haven't been bishops. They internalize it (with the help of the adversary) as a clear message from God that they don't have what it takes, and they must not have been obedient enough to qualify for such a position. I have even heard stories from men who have served as bishops but now beat themselves up because they were "looked over" for a position in a stake presidency. I am sure many reading this are thinking, *Not me; I've never wanted to be a bishop or have a demanding calling.* That might be the case, but you have still sought out acceptance in other areas of life, whether from a job promotion, how you show up for your parents or children, how well you can maintain your home, your perceived life on social media. The thirst for acceptance is part of our human nature. We chase titles, accolades, and promotions because we crave acceptance. We crave acceptance because we have a wound that hurts and needs to be numbed. Being the "nice guy" isn't going to remove God's disappointment in you—it was never there in the first place. He accepted you the day He created you, and He accepts you today. Nothing has changed.

Numbing Through Sin

By now, you can see the effectiveness of numbing through a façade. Another effective way to numb a wound is through sin. We saw a glimpse of this in Brad's story. The argument with his wife triggered his wound, so he numbed it by viewing pornography.

When I served as a bishop, a single man in his thirties came to meet with me. He had met with several bishops before about a recurring problem with masturbation. We had several lively, Spirit-filled discussions that built trust between the two of us. He got to the point where he felt safe confiding in me that he had been sexually abused repeatedly as a child. My heart broke for him as he tearfully shared this tragic wound he had been suffering with for years and years. I pled with him to seek professional counseling to help him deal with the trauma this had caused. I offered to cover any expense with fast-offering funds to make sure he got the necessary therapy. No matter how much I pled, he refused. His way of dealing with this wound—and any stress that caused it to flare up—was to numb it through masturbation. This cycle is very common with other compulsions or addictions. Often as a bishop, when someone would confess a struggle with pornography, I would, unfortunately, hyper-focus on the negative behavior. I would increase accountability, suggest internet filters, and restrict ordinances— all in an attempt to motivate them to stop the negative behavior.

IS GOD DISAPPOINTED IN ME?

I didn't realize that these individuals weren't just acting out to act out. They were numbing a wound they didn't know how to reconcile. I would have served these individuals much better and caused less secondary shame if I would have sought out the wound in their hearts rather than focus on the behavior.

Sin has a euphoric effect on our minds, especially related to sins that involve natural or unnatural chemicals. Sexual sin releases natural chemicals in the brain like dopamine and oxytocin, giving a feeling of happiness and comfort, exactly what the wound ordered. The problem with this solution is that it is very temporary and requires the person to return to these activities, which can form compulsive behavior or addiction. These numbing activities can also numb the feelings these chemicals produce, which is why you will see sex or drug addicts turn to more intense forms of acting out to reach the same level of numbing. Now, I wouldn't go so far as to claim that every form of sinning will turn into an addiction, but when we understand the wound and the numbing that is required it is not surprising to see why nearly all addictions develop from some type of wound.

Façades and sinning are not mutually exclusive. More often than not, individuals will use both façades and sinning to find the level of relief they need to numb their wounds. When wounds lead to positive or righteous behavior, we don't see the problem on the surface. Isn't that a good thing? Shouldn't anything that promotes positive behaviors be encouraged? Not when wounds are involved. Remember Steve from the last chapter, who was living a double life? Not only was he numbing his wound by acting out sexually, but he was also numbing his wound through positive behaviors. He served in a bishopric and as a temple worker, hoping his positive, righteous behaviors would

121

outweigh the harm of living a double life. These righteous behaviors helped him feel acceptance from his wife, family, and church leaders, but he was only hiding the wound behind a façade while he numbed the wound with sin. It's more common than you might realize. Since Steve has reached recovery, he has started a passion project called Unashamed Unafraid, a nonprofit organization and podcast where he records the stories of men who have reached recovery from sexual addiction through Christ. After listening to several of those stories, you hear a pattern of men who dealt with their wounds by sinning and magnifying righteous façades through diligent efforts in their callings or Church attendance.

Spiritual System Reset

Façades and sinning to numb can distort a personal spiritual journey so much that a simple change of behaviors isn't enough. Not only does an individual need to repent, but they need an entire jumpstart to their system. This is where things can get messy because people find this reset in a variety of ways. For someone like Steve, just saying sorry and promising to never do it again wasn't what his system needed. He needed a full reset, which came through the process of a membership council where his Church membership was removed. This wasn't done to be mean to Steve or to punish him. It was an action of reset. It was time to remove all blessings and covenant promises from Steve so that he could reset his system from the ground up with the help of the Savior and then, later on, approach those covenants again with a sound foundation.

Other individuals take a different path. Their false premise of a gospel that is too heavy on behaviors and always wanting more doesn't heal their wounds, and they make the false assumption that

IS GOD DISAPPOINTED IN ME?

the gospel itself is what is doing all the hurting. They then intentionally step away from the gospel. For some individuals, having such a contorted view of the gospel or assuming God is disappointed in them leads them to feel that, like Steve, they need time away from the blessings and covenant promises of the gospel because it is built on such a false premise. From the perspective of our religious community, this is often classified as rebellion, when, in reality, those who are rebellious are simply trying to numb the pain of their wounds caused by overemphasizing behaviors. They, too, need a system reset. These individuals who intentionally step away often are encouraged by the sense of freedom they feel, as they can behave any way that "feels good." They see all those past restrictions and commandments as arbitrary rules that were restricting them from a happier and freer life. However, eventually, they realize happiness is still fleeting, and their wounds continue to hurt. They may fall back on some of their old ways by putting up new façades or even indulging in more sin. At some point, with so much time apart from the gospel, their system will need to reset when they realize they still need Jesus in their life. As they return to seek healing from Him, they will then have to rebuild from the foundation a correct approach to how the gospel serves them in finding healing through the grace of Jesus Christ.

I realize for some people it seems this reset never happens. Their membership is removed from the Church through a formal membership council and they never return, or others abandon the gospel entirely and never return. However, whether in this life or the next, they will at some point come to the realization that only Christ can heal their suffering, and they will need to reach toward Him for a full reset and build their faith from this foundation.

Revisiting the Gospel Continuum

Let's return to the Gospel Continuum we discussed in chapter 3.

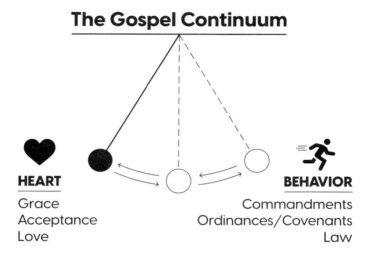

Hiding or numbing wounds—usually by hanging on to the behavior side of the continuum for an extended period of time—becomes exhausting. We expect healing to happen over time, but when it doesn't come, we have one of two options: We can assume the gospel doesn't work and abandon it, or we can surrender the behavior side to the Lord, allowing Him to swing us back to the heart side of the continuum for proper healing. This is scary but is also the beauty of this process because it requires faith in God. This loss of control can propel us into the arms of the Savior, and that is exactly where we find healing. It's called surrender, and it is medicine for the soul. It can all make sense as words on a page, but when it comes to taking the first step of revealing our wounds, it's petrifying, or we don't even know where to begin.

Phillip Yancey, a contemporary Christian author, has talked about this spiritual dynamic and how it is hard for some to admit they are broken and wounded:

> The more unsavory the characters [those willing to surrender their wounds], the more at ease they seemed to feel around Jesus. People like these found Jesus appealing: a Samaritan social outcast, a military officer of the tyrant Herod, a quisling tax collector, a recent hostess to seven demons.
>
> In contrast, Jesus got a chilly response from more respectable types [those clinging to façades]. Pious Pharisees thought him uncouth and worldly, a wealthy young ruler walked away shaking his head, and even the open-minded Nicodemus sought a meeting under cover of darkness. . . . Somehow we have created a community of respectability in the Church. The down-and-out, who flocked to Jesus when he lived on earth, [don't] feel welcome. How did Jesus, the only perfect person in history, manage to attract the notoriously imperfect? And what keeps us from following in his steps today?"[41]

It is our brokenness that will keep us engaged with the Savior. Returning to him again and again for healing keeps us on the path. One of the greatest tragedies of our mortal experience is when the adversary convinces us that we not only need to hide our wounds from the world, but we should also hide them from a God we think is disappointed in us. It is the process of taking our wounds to the Savior that makes us Christian. Elder James R. Rasband said, "Fixing that which you broke and cannot fix is the very purpose of the Atonement of Christ."[42] He wants to heal; we simply must let go of our control and surrender.

Healing in Real Life

If only there was a simple plan that I could type out on the pages of this book so that you know exactly how to heal your wounds. The reality is, you can't heal your wounds from reading a book. Our Father in Heaven has already offered healing by establishing His gospel and sending His Son to atone for our sins and wounds. It's an individual journey that requires you to engage with God and His gospel. That can only be done through your surrender to Jesus Christ, who proclaims, "Behold, I stand at the door, and knock: if any man hear my voice, and open the door, I will come in to him" (Revelation 3:20). In this scriptural imagery, we talk about the door, but we have not defined the door. What would be the doorway of our hearts? It's the wound.

We also learn from Alma 7:11 that Christ "shall go forth, suffering pains and afflictions and temptations of every kind; and this that the word might be fulfilled which saith he will take upon him the pains and the sicknesses of his people," including the wounds. He has suffered for our wounds, but He requires us to open the door to our wounds and invite Him in to heal us. His grace only requires one action from us—that we accept it. Dr. Donald Hilton, author of *He Restoreth My Soul,* writes, "Often when others find out what addiction I have in my life, they want me to name

IS GOD DISAPPOINTED IN ME?

three or four steps to solve the problem so they can help someone they love to find hope and recovery. I can't do that. The only thing I can say is that it takes the Savior to fix it. He is the only one that can resolve it. The only way recovery comes is by total surrender to Him. Complete, total surrender to His way, to His grace, to His benevolence."[43]

Identifying the door to our hearts requires us to discover it, see it, name it, feel it, and then allow Christ to heal it. Think of the blind man in John 9 whom Jesus healed on the Sabbath. The Pharisees interview him to understand what has happened. The blind man doesn't understand it entirely either, but he knows the wound is gone—"One thing I know, that, whereas I was blind, now I see" (John 9:25). But without the wound of being blind, was there anything for Christ to do? Where was the wound that He could heal? If the wound wasn't apparent or identifiable, the healing isn't much of a miracle. If the man was never blind and simply responded, "I was having an 'okay' day, but now I am having a 'pretty good' day," where is the miracle? Where is the transformational nature of the power of the Savior? I love the line from the dramatized television series *The Chosen*.[44] A man asks Mary of Magdalene about her healing, and she responds, "I was one way, and now I am completely different. The thing that happened in between was him. I will know him for the rest of my life."[45] That contrast is so important and impossible to see without an apparent, identified wound. There is no miracle without the wound.

Your first step might be to identify the wounds in your life. Again, if you have nothing for Him to heal, why would you even approach Him? What do you have to surrender to Christ if you can't point to it and label it? This might take days or weeks of reflection. Instead of filling your "daily scripture study" with chapter after chapter, go to the scriptures seeking for the Lord to reveal your brokenness. Where have you hidden it? What façade covers it?

Once you find a wound, you can seek divine direction to surrender the wound. However, you cannot stay in the closet seeking healing from heaven; you have to share the wound with others. Vulnerability is the first step to healing. Sharing the wound with someone you love begins to give the wound air so it can heal. This may require you to open up to a spouse, a friend, a parent, a bishop, or even a professional counselor. During this step, it will be tempting to try to control who knows about the wound, but be open to getting as much help as possible. It may feel like you are losing control, but you are merely transferring control to the Savior.

Share Your Wounds as the Savior Did

When I was a child, my mother had a white porcelain statue of the Christus, a copy of Thorvaldsen's famous sculpture often seen at temple visitor centers, that sat on a shelf in our living room. I remember taking time to admire this statue, looking for the marks on His feet, hands, and side. I had learned about the resurrection of Jesus Christ and often questioned that if He resurrected in a perfect body, why didn't the process heal the wounds in His feet, hands, and side? I later learned about the critical role of those scars. They represented the sacrifice and suffering that He went through for each one of us. Chapter 20 of the book of John recounts the moment that Christ showed His wounds to His disciples, inviting them to witness the evidence of His mission to redeem all mankind. As He is the Perfect Example, I have often wondered if Jesus felt it important to show His wounds so we would learn how to show our own. Often when we get hurt, either physically or spiritually, we hide. We don't want others to know about our hurt, or we are embarrassed that evidence of our hurt will make us appear weak or imperfect. However, there is power in being vulnerable with our wounds. Vulnerability leads to connection, which leads to healing.

If you need a more formal, step-by-step model to healing the wound, you can utilize the Church's Addiction Recovery Program (ARP) manual in the Gospel Library app. The Addiction Recovery Program manual is a remarkable resource. And, if you're seeking healing specifically from an addiction, the ARP hosts meetings for recovering addicts in cities around the world. Visit addictionrecovery.churchofjesuschrist.org for more information.

Unfortunately, the title "Addiction" can make us assume the ARP manual is only for "addicts." I have heard many individuals refer to this book as "The Atonement Implementation Manual." These twelve steps are a powerful way of systematically processing wounds in life and reaching healing. An addiction recovery process is, first and foremost, wound healing. Here are the twelve steps the program will take you through:

Step 1: Honesty

Step 2: Hope

Step 3: Trust in God

Step 4: Truth

Step 5: Confession

Step 6: Change of Heart

Step 7: Humility

Step 8: Seeking Forgiveness

Step 9: Restitution and Reconciliation

Step 10: Daily Accountability

Step 11: Personal Revelation

Step 12: Service

Considering these twelve steps, it is obvious to see the healing nature of this program. If you don't know where to start to find healing through the Savior, try step 1.

Repentance and Healing

For the gospel to be active in our life, we must always be moving in one direction or another on the Gospel Continuum. Wounds are always on the heart, so as we discover the wounds, we must move toward the heart, surrendering our will to receive healing through Christ. We do this each time we discover a wound. It's an ongoing process throughout our lives. The nature of the continuum illustrates the justification, healing, and redemption we experience when we move toward the heart. When we are moving toward the behavior, we are receiving *sanctification*, personal change, and exaltation. Moving on the continuum is a simple way of illustrating repentance. "As we garner sufficient faith and trust to surrender ourselves to the Lord's way meekly, we are repenting."[46] Progress is not found on one side of the continuum or the other—progress is only found as we continually *move* on the continuum. When we stop moving (or get stuck), we stop repenting.

It is often difficult to recognize when we have stopped moving on the continuum. We might get into a daily scripture study routine, weekly temple attendance, and magnifying our calling. We suddenly begin to define ourselves by these behaviors, believing that this is how we earn our love from God. We are suddenly

IS GOD DISAPPOINTED IN ME?

stuck on the behaviors side of the Gospel Continuum. Hopefully, we recognize the additional exhaustion we might be feeling from "living the gospel" and begin to move toward the heart by surrendering any acceptance we are trying to earn to God, being real with those around us, being at peace with the effort we have offered—and, hopefully, we recognize Christ accepts us as we are and will heal us no matter how we behave. Or maybe we have recognized a wound in our life and, through the help of Christ, church leaders, family, and professional therapy, have received healing to the wound. Through the healing we move to the heart side of the continuum; we are then ready to move back toward the continuum's behavior side and receive sanctification through those behaviors. We've learned that we don't need to earn acceptance and feel joy in behaviors through our personal progression.

If you are a parent or bishop, you might discover someone under your care is struggling with sin. It might be tempting to focus on behavior and demand accountability. Now you know the true solution is to help them move toward the gospel of the heart to receive healing and overcome certain behaviors later. A constant focus on behavior change will not stimulate healing. We must focus on the wound.

Maintaining a temple recommend might give us the feeling that we have "arrived" when, in reality, we might be stuck on the behavior side of the continuum. We must discover ways of receiving Christ's grace and move toward the heart so we can continue repenting and progressing.

Godly Disruption

Becoming stuck on the Gospel Continuum can happen so subtly that we can go weeks, months, or even years without realizing we are stuck. Life happens quickly, so we find routines that work for us, and we assume everything is going great. Though wounds exist, we have found a working system to maintain a decent life without worrying about seeking healing for the wounds. God has a way of using disruption in life to unstick us from the continuum so we can progress through repentance. You may think life is right, and there is no need to run off to a therapist's office to search for your brokenness; that is fine for a time, but disruption will find you. When Christ says, "I stand at the door and knock," what He may actually mean is, "I stand at the door and disrupt." It might be through a trial, tribulation, a spiritual awakening, medical diagnosis, or countless other disruptions, but this disruption is what helps us progress and come closer to Him.

My life has been disrupted in a variety of ways. My story about struggling with personal scripture study and the subsequent powerful spiritual interaction at the Christian leadership retreat was one example of a disruption that got me unstuck from within the continuum. I've heard of individuals who have been living a great life and then suddenly received a cancer diagnosis. It causes them to reassess their life and get moving on the continuum to find more profound healing and deeper sanctification. These aren't curses from a vengeful God who is acting out in disappointment. Whether He caused the cancer or not, He is constantly using these disruptions as a way to call you to Him.

Intense wounding can often bring other wounds to the surface, which requires us to reconcile all of them and seek healing. This is a scary process and can often cause some people to leave the Church altogether. I've already shared some of these types of experiences earlier in this chapter.

I recently heard another heartbreaking story about a woman who had lived a very faithful, righteous life. She married in the temple, raised a happy family, and then gave birth to a stillborn child. The doctors had no answers as to why the child was stillborn. This disruption of losing a child unstuck her from the behavior side of the continuum. Still, because her gospel experience never emphasized the heart of the gospel, she saw the gospel as an equation (righteous behaviors + consistency = happiness). She had done all the "right behaviors," so why was God punishing her in this way? She couldn't reconcile this wound and the other wounds that came to the surface, so she left the Church altogether. She thought she was leaving because it "didn't work" when, in reality, she left because leaving was effective in numbing this tragic wound. Like with all of us, Christ is not done with her story. He will continue to pursue her heart and offer her healing. She may have walked away from her covenant journey for now, but Jesus still wants to heal her and will never be disappointed when she seeks that healing.

When we see the full continuum of the gospel—that it is not only a great model for receiving blessings but is also useful in receiving healing—these disruptions can bring us closer to a loving Father rather than encourage us to run away from a disappointed God.

CHAPTER 8

The Raging Love of God

As a young boy, I remember visiting the Lower Falls in Yellowstone National Park. Constructed at the top of this waterfall is an observation deck where people can get close to the raging waters and remain safe. It's hypnotizing to watch so many gallons of water cascade over the mountain and fall several hundred feet to the river below. The sound is deafening! If you throw a rock into the falls, it immediately disappears, consumed by the strength of nature. The gated observation deck would not permit it, but one can imagine the power he would feel by simply putting one hand into the water's velocity. To fully understand the power of Lower Falls, one would also have to stand at the bottom of the falls. Of course, that would overwhelm any human being.

The power of this waterfall is a helpful metaphor for the love of God. Imagine a waterfall representing God's love. Imagine standing on that observation deck. His love is so immense it would, of course, make Lower Falls appear as a dripping kitchen faucet. The strength of God's love is undeniable, especially if one could observe it as a waterfall. The deafening sound of the waterfall alone communicates its strength. This is the power of the heart side of the continuum.

Our desire to feel God's love matches our desire to bask in God's waterfall and absorb as much of it as we can. As we touch it, we want more of it. We touch it with our hands, and then we can't help but dip our toes in. It all feels so good we want to jump in, but we are not capable of receiving it fully. We are torn between the inviting nature of God's love and our inability to soak in it—"For he who is not able to abide the law of a celestial kingdom cannot abide a celestial glory" (Doctrine and Covenants 88:22). We need personal change and exaltation to become beings capable of receiving more of His love. Thankfully, His love propels us toward the opposite side of the continuum by considering behaviors, covenants, and commandments so we can become more like Him and have the strength to step deeper into His love. As Christ taught, "As the Father hath loved me, so have I loved you: continue ye in my love. If ye keep my commandments, ye shall abide in my love; even as I have kept my Father's commandments, and abide in his love" (John 15:9–10).

Becoming Able to Abide in His Love

Elder D. Todd Christofferson has said, "To 'continue in' or 'abide in' the Savior's love means to receive His grace and be perfected by it. To receive His grace, we must have faith in Jesus Christ and keep His commandments, including repenting of our sins, being baptized for the remission of sins, receiving the Holy Ghost, and continuing on the path of obedience."[47] We've learned that swinging toward God's love creates momentum that propels us toward righteous behaviors; similar momentum is created when we swing deep into behaviors, commandments, and covenants. As long as we avoid the overwhelm of behaviors by not getting stuck there,

IS GOD DISAPPOINTED IN ME?

we maintain the momentum necessary to swing back toward God's love and reach a deeper part of those raging waters.

An individual may stand on the banks of God's raging love and soak in the love as much as possible. They may enjoy it so much that they never want to leave. Naturally, they will want to feel even more of His love and may demand that God let them step farther into the moving water. However, certain behaviors required to go deeper may seem too much of a sacrifice and too hard. They demand, "Father! You love me. Let me walk out and experience more of your love." The more they try, the more apparent it is that they are simply incapable of absorbing more of God's love. President Russell M. Nelson has taught, "The resplendent bouquet of God's love—including eternal life—includes blessings for which we must qualify, not entitlements to be expected unworthily. Sinners cannot bend His will to theirs and require Him to bless them in sin (Alma 11:37). If they desire to enjoy every bloom in His beautiful bouquet, they must repent."[48] Repentance is pivotal in the process of abiding in more of God's love. In other words, we must always be moving either toward heart or behavior on the continuum. God loves to see His children approach the banks of His love and dip their toes in, but He has more for us to experience. He just needs us to become more able to abide in His love. Elder Dieter F. Uchtdorf taught this principle when he testified, "The grace of God does not merely restore us to our previous innocent state. . . . His aim is much higher: He wants His sons and daughters to become like Him."[49] As we run toward the love of God, it gives us greater momentum to run back toward commandments. As we engage more deeply in commandments, it gives us greater strength to move toward God's deeper love.

Is God's Love Conditional?

This is where a tragic misunderstanding about God's love can take place. We assume that because we have to turn to behaviors, covenants, and commandments to more deeply *abide* in God's love, we assume this is a process of *earning* God's love or that God restricts His love from us until we behave a certain way. God never restricts His love. He will never diminish the force of His love depending on our behaviors. On tough days when it has been hard for us to live up to commandments and covenants, we will not return to the waterfall of love and find only a drizzle. When we are desperate for God's love during those tough days, we can return to His waterfall and find it raging just the same. It will speak to us, as if to say, *My love is still here! It will always be here! Come bask in it as much as you can until you feel ready to return to my commandments and try again. We will figure this out together, and you will be amazed at what you become and how much of My love you can enjoy.*

In a world full of hyperbole and platitudes, it's common to hear the concept that God's love is unconditional or that a parent's love for a child should be unconditional. Stephen Robinson stated in his book *Following Christ*, "There has been a great deal of discussion about God's 'unconditional' love lately, and most of the discussion has not been very useful. If God is love, and if the prime directive is to love as God loves, then is God's love 'unconditional,' and should mine also be 'unconditional'? That is a loaded question, for unconditional means different things to different people, and the core of the misunderstanding lies in those different definitions."[50]

Stating God's love is *conditional* or *unconditional* leads to assumptions. For example, what feelings come to mind when you think about unconditional love? Perhaps safety, acceptance, or grace? What feelings come to mind when you think about conditional love? Maybe abandonment, manipulation, needing to earn the love, or feelings of shame?

So, if we feel that God's love is conditional, we assume He is retracting love depending on our actions or that He will abandon us unless we do exactly what He wants. Where is the grace in that? It feels manipulative and more punishment focused. Let's look at another analogy to understand the nature of God's love better.

Consider a family that has two twin teenage sisters. One sister is generally obedient to family rules, and the other sister is more rebellious. The parents have the same amount of love for each one, but one seems always to be slamming doors and sneaking out with friends, and the other has more privilege and freedom because of her general respect for her parents and the boundaries they have set. The obedient daughter, though not perfect, enjoys a deeper level of access to her parents' hearts as they have a regular game night routine together where they laugh and connect as a family. Their other daughter has built resentment and hates being in the same room as her parents. She retracts from her parents and only shows herself when she needs something to eat or is hurrying out the door to hang out with friends. The rebellious daughter is continually reminding her parents that they love the other daughter more than her since the "good girl" has fewer restrictions and more access to them. Every time the parents hear her say this, it breaks their hearts. The parents spend time every night desperately praying for this daughter to open up and access the incredible love they have for her. The parents' level of love for both daughters is raging like a mighty waterfall. It is immeasurable and freely given, but the

KURT FRANCOM

daughters' abilities to access it are quite different. Obedience doesn't increase love; it increases access.

Some scriptures can give the impression that God is so disappointed in you that He will limit His love: "And as pertaining to the new and everlasting covenant, it was instituted for the fulness of my glory; and he that receiveth a fulness thereof must and shall abide the law, or he shall be damned, saith the Lord God" (Doctrine and Covenants 132:6); "If you keep not my commandments, the love of the Father shall not continue with you, therefore you shall walk in darkness" (Doctrine and Covenants 95:12); "But in every nation he that feareth him, and worketh righteousness, is accepted with him" (Acts 10:35). Reading scriptures like these in the wrong tone can cause us to assume God is on His way to "damn" us if we are not doing what He asks or that He will punish us by not loving us anymore. The reality is, God isn't the one damning us or restricting the deeper parts of His love; we do that ourselves. The adversary convinces us that if we even try to visit the waterfall of God's love, we will find it dried up. However, "God's love is there for you whether or not you feel you deserve love. It is simply always there."[51] Is God's raging love conditional? No. Do we restrict ourselves from His love, making it feel conditional? Yes.

Even President Nelson has assured us of this love. Speaking in the context that we sometimes restrict or damn ourselves from God's love, he said this:

> Does this mean the Lord does not love the sinner? Of course not. Divine love is infinite and universal. The Savior loves both the saints and the sinners. The Apostle John affirmed, "We love him, because he first loved us." And Nephi, upon seeing in vision the Lord's

mortal ministry, declared: "The world, because of their iniquity, shall judge him to be a thing of naught; wherefore they scourge him, and he suffereth it; and they smite him, and he suffereth it. Yea, they spit upon him, and he suffereth it, because of his loving kindness and his long-suffering towards the children of men." We know the expansiveness of the Redeemer's love because He died that all who die might live again.[52]

Again, like a pendulum, the more we progress on the behaviors side of the continuum the more momentum we have when we swing back to the heart or love side of the continuum. As we repent or move in one direction or the other on the continuum, we are building up more and more force to not only benefit from the deeper parts of God's love but to also benefit from the deeper parts of His covenants, because "God's greater blessings are conditioned on obedience."[53] He will always be pleading for His children to step deeper into His love. That deafening sound of His plea will never diminish, no matter what we do or don't do in life.

Conditional Blessings

When we consider the Gospel Continuum, the same amount of love is available no matter where you find yourself. Whether you are excelling at establishing routines of righteous behavior or are struggling to find self-worth or repentance in your gospel journey, God loves you the same. However, we find various levels of blessings at different parts of the continuum. This is where the adversary inserts his favorite lies. He wants us to equate blessings with love. There are many incredible blessings given through grace, with no behavioral expectation from us on the heart side of the continuum.

For example, Jesus gave us the incredible blessing of salvation. Your ticket to heaven is already paid for; you simply have to pick it up from will-call. Christ justifies us at no extra cost to us. Part of that justification is the resurrection we will all experience someday—again, at no cost.

Then there are additional blessings available if we are willing to behave righteously. Elder Christofferson has said, "God's greater blessings are conditioned on obedience."[54] Or in other words, God's greater blessings are found on the covenant side of the continuum. After receiving so many blessings through grace we might be discouraged when these greater blessings are not given freely. *God, you let me wade into your waterfall of love near the shore, so why don't you allow me to walk into your greater blessings freely? Are you restricting that love from me?* This is when the adversary uses these conditional blessings as proof that God's love *is* conditional. It is a lie. Just like the twin teenage daughter was given many blessings from her parents freely, some of the greater blessings that her obedient sister was experiencing were only available because she had taken steps of "righteousness" or "right relationship," as we discussed in chapter 5. Because she had created a "right relationship" with her parents, she enabled herself to become the person capable of walking deeper into her parents' love. The parents continue to beg their wayward daughter to act in a way that will give her access to the deeper love of a "right relationship." Still, the daughter interprets it as parents withdrawing love when, in reality, she is withdrawing herself from the love available to her.

My friend Ty Mansfield tells the story of when he was a young college student grappling with same-sex attraction. He had a deep desire to stay within the Church and respect the covenants he had made, but over time he wondered if that was the best path for him to take. Could he find stability and happiness by avoiding the same-sex relationships that felt so natural to him? He finally decided that he would begin dating other men to see if that path offered the most happiness for him. After driving home from one specific date with a man he had been regularly seeing, he suddenly felt a remarkable feeling of love pass over him. God knew of his situation and the struggle he was going through. It would be easy to assume God would restrict his love since Ty was beginning down a path that wasn't in line with his covenants. But instead, God met Ty with an enormous amount of love. This was a prominent moment in Ty's life that influenced him to swing back toward the covenant side of the continuum. Ty needed heart and love, not a divine reprimand. Through feeling God's love, Ty was reminded that greater blessings were available to him through a covenant path. God wasn't restricting those blessings, but Ty had the power to restrict *himself* from God's deeper relationship and blessings. We must never misinterpret our choice to restrict ourselves from God's greater blessings and deeper relationship.

I have felt this reminder of incredible love in my own life. On those busy, exhausting weeks when I feel so far behind or feel like I could have done so much better, the Lord seems to remind me, *I love you. I'm right here. Keep going, and you'll figure this out.* A disappointed God would only magnify the weight of exhaustion. Thankfully, our God will always help us carry it and encourage us on.

God Loves Effort

Keeping those covenants sanctifies and blesses us in ways that would not be possible without our effort. This is why President Nelson said, "The Lord loves effort."[55] These greater blessings that come through effort sanctify us and help us become more like God. As we return to the heart side of the continuum, we can now go deeper into the waterfall of God's raging love.

Even though effort is involved in this sanctifying process, it should never outshine grace. I remember a time in my life when I was running a web-development company. I would contact small businesses in my city and offer to build them a website to help them increase their business success. I remember one particular client that took a lot of effort to win over. Over twelve months, I consistently reached out to him, offering him promotions, extra services, and anything else I could think of to convince him to sign up with our web services. Finally, after much persistence, he agreed to become our client. During that same time, I had multiple clients simply call me up and immediately sign up for our services without requiring much effort. So the question is, which blessing of a new client came by grace, and which one came by effort? The reality is, they both came by grace. Even when we show effort, it may feel like we are earning something, but every blessing is a gift. Every blessing is made possible by the infinite sacrifice of Jesus Christ. However, effort must be part of the process—not to earn God's love, but to become something greater. How can we learn never to give up if we don't have an experience that tempts us to give up? Sure, God could mold us into perfect people with His unlimited strength, but the fire of effort makes us stronger.

Faith in Outcomes

We typically relate blessings to specific outcomes. The single sister in her thirties hopes for the blessing of marriage to experience the outcome of a traditional family and children. The exhausted parents of toddlers hope for the blessing of children who serve missions and marry in the temple so they can experience the outcomes of a blessed life of happiness. It's so easy to pore over a patriarchal blessing searching for the promised outcomes that will make life more comfortable or worth it. In our search for spiritual lottery tickets, we fail to realize our goal is to come unto Christ rather than merely come unto blessings.

Blake Fisher works at BYU as an inclusion counselor. His job requires him to create space for LGBTQ Latter-day Saints on campus who might need someone to talk to about their college or religious experience while being LGBTQ. He has shared with me how many of the individuals he has worked with are holding more faith in outcomes than they are in Jesus Christ. Some put all their faith in a possible temple marriage and a happy Latter-day Saint family. Others put all their faith in the hope that the Church will adjust doctrine or procedures to make same-sex marriage available to them in the temple. He has found the most stability and contentment in those individuals who have set their focus on Christ regardless of what blessings or outcomes they expect.

We all do it. We will all catch ourselves in a moment when we are working toward an outcome rather than a relationship with Christ. Author Adam Miller has said, "Work, chained to its outcome, is misery. Do what you can, do it better than you're able, and let things happen as they may. The action, not its fruit, is your business. The outcome is not your concern."[56] Engaging and moving on the Gospel Continuum is the action that will deepen our relationship with Christ.

Grace and Disappointment Cannot Coexist

Our attempt to love God first so He will then love us back is a mental prison the adversary convinces us to step into. It is impossible for us to love Him first because "He first loved us" (1 John 4:19). Our

Eternal Father accepted us the day He created us. He didn't send us here to Earth to see if we could make His team; He sent us here because we are already on His team. "For God so loved the world" first . . . and then "sent His Son" (John 3:16). He never intended to send His Son to change us into something lovable. He loved us first and then sent His Son, who could help change us into someone like Him. We are His, and He will never close the door on us, because He has never been disappointed in us.

During the First Vision, God explained to Joseph Smith that all other "creeds were an abomination in his sight; that those professors were all corrupt; that: 'they draw near to me with their lips, but their hearts are far from me, they teach for doctrines the commandments of men, having a form of godliness, but they deny the power thereof'" (Joseph Smith—History 1:19). Very similarly, we can fall into the same trap. It feels like we are drawing nearer to God with our lips, or the things we say. Sometimes we focus on "doctrines of devils, or the commandments of men" (Doctrine and Covenants 46:7), like believing in a disappointed God. This causes our *hearts* to go far from God and "deny the power thereof," which is God's love. Never deny that infinite, ongoing power that encourages us on.

It is impossible for our Father in Heaven to be full of grace and also disappointed. God accepts us as we are. Adam Miller put it this way:

> Love is for its own sake. It works only as a gift, never as a reward. It can't be earned or bartered, or insured. It is a grace, and it is freely given or not given at all. Uncouple your desire to be loved from your desire to be great. Pursue love by striving to give it rather than

IS GOD DISAPPOINTED IN ME?

possessing it. Coupling love and ambition fools us into approaching the whole business backward. Rather than pursuing love by giving ourselves away, we end up trying to capture love with a new and improved version of ourselves. This sucks the freedom out of love, and it sucks the joy out of excellence.[57]

I think Jesus puts it best in His own words:

O all ye that are . . . more righteous, will ye not now return unto me, and repent of your sins, and be converted, that I may heal you?   Yea, verily I say unto you, if ye will come unto me ye shall have eternal life. Behold, mine arm of mercy is extended towards you, and whosoever will come, him will I receive; and blessed are those who come unto me. Behold, I am Jesus Christ the Son of God. I created the heavens and the earth, and all things that in them are. I was with the Father from the beginning. I am in the Father, and the Father in me; and in me hath the Father glorified his name. (3 Nephi 9:13–15)

God is begging us to receive the power of His love. We are His righteous people, or His people in the "right relationship." There is no shame in repenting of our sins. There is no slammed door in our faces—no rejection. The power of His love will heal us. He is proactive in offering His mercy; we just have to accept it. He created the heavens and Earth and everything that exists; He created you; He can transform you. *That* is the power of the raging love of God.

CHAPTER 9

Grace for Grace

Christ "received not of the fulness at the first, but received grace for grace" (Doctrine and Covenants 93:12). When we reject shame, embrace our divine identity, and open our hearts to the incredible grace coming from God, a glorious cycle begins. Not only do we grow and develop as we *receive* grace from God, but also as we *give* grace to others. We receive grace-filled covenants because we believe God loves us; in turn, we become people who can give more grace to others; and that grace we extend to others, in turn, enables us to better receive God's grace—grace for grace! Rephrased, experiencing God's love for us enables us to act more like Him in our daily interactions—loving others more fully regardless of their behaviors and minimizing the disappointment in our own relationships—and also enables us to receive a greater fulness of God's grace into our soul. We become people who are less disappointed in others, and this helps us believe in a God who is never disappointed in us. This is the cycle of grace for grace!

Unfortunately, being a mortal is tough. We like the idea of giving grace in return for grace, but we typically end up giving *expectations* for *outcomes*. Yes, we would love to be as patient and loving as our Eternal Father, but we are desperate to see "progress" in life—especially in the lives of those we care about the most.

Focusing Only on Outcomes

At the time of this writing, my son is five years old. As his parent, I have so much ambition for him. I want him to succeed and find deep happiness in life. I can close my eyes and see it so clearly. It's 2034, and we are standing outside the Provo MTC. My son is dressed in a brand-new suit, hugging his siblings with tears in his eyes. I can almost feel the anxiety of leaving my son there as he starts a remarkable two years. I like to suppose he is preparing for a Spanish-speaking mission in Sacramento, California, since that is where my beloved mission happened. I'm excited for my son to experience the same life-changing moments a mission offered me.

But what if he doesn't serve a mission? It's something I desperately want for my son. Naturally, I double down my efforts by infusing his life with more and more behaviors. I want to will his mission into existence. Instead of offering grace for grace, I offer my son an *expectation* for an *outcome*. If the time comes to serve and he doesn't offer the outcome of serving a mission, I imagine I'll naturally be inclined to offer disappointment.

What if, instead, I offered grace? What if I continue to share with him the joys and blessings of my mission, but I let go of the expectation for him to serve his own mission? By offering that grace to him, what will it do for our relationship? Will he want to be closer to me? Will he want to be more like me? Or will it cause him to be more casual about his commitment to the gospel? I can't control my son's actions; I simply want to be more like the Great Grace Giver. But how?

As mortals, we have a weakness related to expectations and outcomes because, unlike God, we are not all knowing and are still learning to embrace a full conviction of Christ's Atonement. This makes it more natural to hyperfocus on the gospel equation and reach for outcomes because we assume doing certain behaviors is what brings happiness and blessings (righteousness + consistency = change of heart). *If I can only figure out how to convince my son to serve a mission, then he will more fully embrace the gospel, marry in the temple, and live a much happier and blessed life.* But what about all the other people who didn't serve missions and still live happy and blessed lives? If I only offer expectations and lean on outcomes to bless the life of my son, I'm not trusting the playbook God is using with my son. In addition, I remove grace from our relationship. It becomes transactional and empty, even with my best intentions to bless my son's life.

As I have explored this principle with other parents, they voice the feeling that I am trying to remove the one super-tool that has helped them motivate their children. Often, they can think of countless examples where they set a clear and ambitious expectation for their children, and it did cause them to work harder to achieve it. However, just because shame works doesn't mean we should use it. Shame is motivating in the short term but is a relationship cancer. More on this in the next chapter.

It's easy to double down on pushing expectations to get desired outcomes because we assume it is specific outcomes that stimulate a change of heart. I speak from firsthand experience when I say a mission changed me. That is the nature of doing hard things— being committed to long days walking the streets of Sacramento or attempting to speak Spanish for twenty-four months was transformational. However, a mission isn't the only "hard thing" that will stimulate growth. The goal isn't to push people into hard things; the goal is to establish a relationship they can turn to when they need help as they grapple with those hard things. If a child only expects to find disappointment in the eyes of a parent because of a failed outcome, they most likely won't look for help in that transactional relationship.

When we remind those we love about our personal priority on specific expectations and outcomes in their life (mission, temple marriage, etc.) we establish a scorecard of expectations, which turns into a scorecard of identity. If my son begins to gauge his identity by whether he serves a mission or not, he may assume God is doing the same. When he doesn't live up to that expectation, he may begin to wonder (with the help of the adversary) if there is something wrong with him since he is not measuring up to expectations.

When we inflict those we love with the shame of expectations, naturally that shame splashes back on us and impacts our own perceived identity. We get stuck on the behavior side of our own Gospel Continuum. For example, if an adult child has a drug addiction surface, we might consider the cause to be our lack of consistent family scripture study during their early teenage years. We see our child reconsidering his desire to serve a mission, and we might think we didn't bear our testimony to him enough. We feel the need to fix these problems through behavior change, and that only leads to offering more and more expectations. We fail to see that we actually need to swing the relationship with our child toward love and grace and, in doing so, encourage them to naturally build momentum toward positive behaviors—not because they are *expected* to do so, but because they want to do so.

It feels difficult to not constantly offer expectations for outcomes because God entrusted us with influence over His children. We simply want to do our job of giving them the best chance at eternal life. However, God is not an expectation-dealing parent. He is not offering an expectation—He is offering us grace. He doesn't expect us to make our loved ones perfect when He has already assigned that job to Christ. He offers us grace so that *we* can offer grace and, in return, receive more grace from Him. Grace for grace!

Expectation Pain

Renowned Latter-day Saint life coach Jody Moore explains that focusing on outcomes leads to expectation pain. We love others so much, and, naturally, we develop expectations for them in order to make sure they are successful and happy. We feel a level of pain or discontentment when others don't embrace the expectations we have set for them. That pain isn't their fault for not embracing our expectations; it is our own fault for giving them expectations in the first place. They may not see the value in our desired outcomes. This is an easy mistake to make early on in parenting. Our developing children don't yet understand how to hold their own personal expectations, so we get used to doing it for them. A grandfather may notice that a granddaughter, who is approaching high school graduation, has not yet filled out any college applications. He assumes her sweet, still-developing brain doesn't yet understand how difficult life can be in adulthood without a solid education. She has not yet considered how important it is to stay on top of the college-application process. She is proving to be unable to hold that expectation for herself, so her grandfather decides to hold that expectation for her. In his effort to develop a relationship with his granddaughter, he adheres to the expectation of college, which instead can become a sticking point that impedes the development of the relationship and leads to resentment. There can be no exchange of grace because no space for grace was created. That space is too full of expectation.

Or a wife of a husband who struggles with pornography can't understand why her husband continues to relapse. She has made it clear that she has an expectation that porn use does not happen in their relationship, so in an effort to help him, she begins to hold on to expectation for him and remind him of addiction recovery meeting times, even driving him to the meeting location. She prods him to do his daily practice homework so that he stays clean. She has a clear expectation she is offering him and expects a certain outcome. The issue is, it begins to define their relationship and crowds out the space for love and grace.

Now, a relationship like this where a husband is struggling with pornography definitely needs strong boundaries in order to create safety and trust for all involved. She should create strong boundaries and hold fast to them. However, if she does so only to force a specific outcome it won't have the power to build a relationship worth having even if he reaches sobriety. Manipulating others to act in a certain way that creates a specific outcome is called co-dependency. It requires little surrender and doesn't create healthy relationships.

When we attempt to navigate our relationships by offering expectations and waiting for specific outcomes, we create no space for full acceptance and love. We become like the figure skater attempting to qualify for the Olympics while still holding onto the ice rink wall. The wall guarantees us the outcome of not falling, but it holds us back from connecting with the center of the ice, where the real growth happens. It is by surrendering outcomes that we find deep connection in our relationships and can more fully offer grace to our loved ones and receive grace from God.

When we consider being "faithful" to God we typically think that means we need to behave in a certain way to demonstrate our faith. Though that is part of faithfulness, having faith in Jesus Christ also means we show confidence in His divine sacrifice by surrendering all expectations to Him and trusting He will do the saving. That is why God can so easily set outcome and expectation apart

IS GOD DISAPPOINTED IN ME?

from our relationship with Him. God knows that "[Christ's] grace is sufficient" (2 Corinthians 12:9). God has full faith in Christ! Therefore, the expectations are nonexistent. He has the same ability and capacity to love the addict in the gutter as He does the bishop on the stand. Our Redeemer removed the sting of eternal damnation, so God is never held back by outcome or expectation. That is grace. Because God can sit with us in infinite love no matter where we are in life, He also has the power to redeem us the moment we mumble the word "Help" from the gutter.

A Foundation of Relationship

There is no doubt that individuals can make decisions that lead to terrible outcomes. Sin should be taken very seriously because all sin leads to personal destruction. "But behold, I say unto you that if ye persist in your wickedness . . . ye shall be visited with utter destruction" (Alma 9:18). The problem arises when we hold so much expectation for others that when they do begin to destroy their life through sin or poor choices, there is no relationship left to stimulate love and repentance. In Luke 15, the prodigal son assumed he would find a father ready to preach a lecture. *I told you so. If you only did what I expected. You must now be my servant!* In our attempt to hold back grace in order to nudge people we love down a specific path of expectations, we end up destroying the relationship they need most when they are "a great way off," ready to turn around and repent (Luke 15:20). Let us, rather, be like the father to the prodigal son and run to our wayward loved-ones, have compassion on them, and give them our best robes, rings, and shoes. Nothing is more motivating than grace. God sets aside outcome and expectation, and this stimulates the type of relationship with us that allows us to ask for help when we are struggling the most;

especially when we need repentance the most. It's the relationship, not the outcome, that fuels redemption. We can follow the same pattern with our own loved ones.

As children of God we are all born with the innate desire to become something more—to become like our Father in Heaven. We don't have to force this expectation into the hearts of our loved ones; they already possess it. We can help free that desire by offering love and acceptance first. Stephen Covey once said, "If we want to help our children or other people change their behavior, we begin by improving the quality of our relationships with them. And we introduce new ideas before we introduce new expectations and controls. In other words, we help them see the world differently. When a person's paradigm changes, everything else changes with it."[58]

This is a concept I wrestle with every day, especially as a parent. This is the epitome of "easier said than done." But this wrestle shifts my focus and changes my prayers. Instead of praying for specific outcomes in the lives of those I love and lead, I suddenly seek for the power to offer grace. *Help me, Father, to accept my brother for where he is and not push my outcomes on him. Will you help me trust Your grace? Help me feel Your acceptance by enabling me to find full acceptance of my brother.* Remember, God is not disappointed in your constant focus on expectations and outcomes because Jesus's sacrifice covers your weakness too. It is natural to desire outcomes, but I hope we take the time to sit with these questions and ponder why we make outcomes such a priority in our relationships with others. There is a deeper process happening that we may not see.

The Identity Battle in Our Personal Relationships

Just like most things, the adversary uses outcomes against us. As mentioned in chapter 4, he wants us to seek validation from other

IS GOD DISAPPOINTED IN ME?

sources, including our relationships with loved ones. The outcomes and actions of those we love can sometimes influence how we perceive our own identity. As parents struggle with their own wounds and inadequacies, they look to hide behind their children's positive behaviors and accomplishments. Or they feel shame as their children act out in ways that expose their own wounds and inadequacies. They not only feel personally broken, but their family feels broken as well. They feel exposed, and it perpetuates their own perceived negative identity. Consider how vulnerable a parent is when their child decides not to serve a mission in a culture that strongly promotes the expectation of missionary service. It's difficult for that parent to not question their identity as a parent.

During the time my two brothers and I all concurrently served as bishops of our respective wards, I invited my mother to my ward for Mother's Day. One sister, a young mother of boys, approached my mother and shared how impressed she was that my mom had three sons serving as bishops. She then asked my mom what her secret was. How did she figure out how to raise boys who would be trusted to be bishops later in life? My mom had no answer for her. There is no parenting strategy or step-by-step plan that guarantees a righteous priesthood holder's development, nor is the outcome of a specific calling proof that a parent set the perfect expectation. While my siblings and I experienced remarkable parenting and love growing up in our home, I am sure other households with the same love and nourishment end up with very different outcomes.

We also live in a world obsessed with outcomes in all areas of life (school, career, sports, etc.). Outcomes can feel like proof that a stable relationship has happened between the child and God, and, therefore, our children will be happier and have less to worry about. However, we can all think of someone who has achieved "successful outcomes" but suffers from terrible relationships. Was it worth it? When we focus on outcomes, relationships become contingent on behaviors and begin to decay from shame. This goes for our relationship with God and our relationships with each other. We must not focus on obtaining "desired outcomes" in life at the expense of forging a relationship with God.

Heavenly Father, Earthly Father

It's remarkable how relationships around us, especially our parental relationships, can influence our understanding of who our Heavenly Father is (both correctly and incorrectly). In our mortal experience, we are continually striving to understand the world around us, especially at a young age. When we taste something new, we often compare it to something else we have already tasted. *It tastes like chicken!* When we begin to establish our fashion style in high school, we often look at how our peers dress. We have a front-row seat to our parents' style of parenting, so when it comes to understanding our Eternal Father in Heaven, we assume He is much like our earthly father or mother. We hopefully know what it's like to be cuddled by them, encouraged by them, and, of course, we have all seen sternness in their eyes when they are flustered, upset, and even disappointed. So, is God like our parents?

As we develop as young children, we experience certain discomforts and even traumas that create triggers in us. These triggers lead to a psychological phenomenon called *projection*. I'm no psychologist, and I don't intend to give you a comprehensive explanation of this phenomenon. Still, I think a basic understanding of this is essential to fully understand how our perception of our Father in

IS GOD DISAPPOINTED IN ME?

Heaven is formed. When our parent yells and condemns us to time out we begin to make assumptions about what all parental relationships look like. We begin to define parental love as very conditional: sometimes it is there, and other times, when I am misbehaving, love is absent. Our parental definition becomes concrete, and then we project it on all other parental interactions, including those with our Heavenly Father.

Maybe when you were growing up, each time you broke curfew, one of your parents huffed and puffed as they paced the living room waiting for your return. You knew grounding and other sharp consequences would follow, and you now unconsciously link bad behaviors to negative consequences, and negative consequences to perceived retraction of parental love. Now in life, when you break a commandment, you assume God is huffing and puffing in His heavenly living room, ready to send negative consequences your way. This cycle of behaviors and projection cripples personal identity. Between how our parents parented us and what they taught us about God, we naturally project many different behaviors and character traits onto our Heavenly Father. This can be a good thing if our father or mother was loving, kind, and full of grace, but what if he or she was mostly grumpy, dismissive, or even abusive? It has a dramatic and long-lasting impact on how children and adults perceive God.

Well-known Christian author William Paul Young said, "It took me 50 years to wipe the face of my father off the face of God."[59] For many of us, we haven't even considered how we have projected the face of our father or mother onto the face of God. We do it unconsciously. After years of experiencing a parent who primarily offers us expectations in exchange for outcomes, it is natural to assume God parents the same way. We may have concluded God is a disappointed God simply because we have disappointed parents.

As we give God the opportunity to correct our false assumptions about His identity, we allow Him to correct the false assumptions we have of our own eternal identity. We have to remove the face of our earthly father or mother from His face to more deeply know Him and love Him. By doing this we give Him grace, and then we recognize the grace He has been giving us from the beginning.

The Disappointed Parent

One day after I'd finished teaching these concepts to a group of married graduate students in a ward near the University of Utah, a young, tired mother approached me and said, "What about me? As a mother, I am constantly disappointed with my children. Is that a bad thing?" My heart broke for this mother, who no doubt was desperately striving to be a great mother and raise wonderful children. Is it wrong to be disappointed as a parent? That's like asking, is it wrong if you get sick, tempted, or hungry?

Disappointment is part of our mortal experience. It's important to recognize those feelings while not letting the shame of those feelings define us. Even as the author of this book, I still experience disappointment in my children. I still struggle with offering expectations to my children and expecting certain outcomes in return. As I learn and grow in the gospel, and as I get better at more fully understanding the Atonement of Jesus Christ, I can more easily surrender outcomes to God, knowing that Jesus has zeroed out all outcomes. I can then begin to remove disappointment from my relationships with others, especially with my children.

IS GOD DISAPPOINTED IN ME?

Progress on this front is possible, and we can help those we love better understand that the face of God is not our face, our reactions are not always His reactions, and our love is strong but not yet as strong as our Eternal Creator's. We can lead them to a more accepting, loving Eternal Parent who deeply desires to help them through mortality and define them as they are—a child of God.

CHAPTER 10

Leading with Love

The argument against relationships based on behavior and outcomes can be a tough one for some to embrace. There are parents with decades of experience (much more than I have) who can look back at their families and think, *I pushed behaviors for most of my children's lives, and it seemed to work.* That's one of the hardest parts about relationships in mortality—shame is reliable and effective, and it works to get a desired outcome. That's why the adversary uses it so much.

Well, wait a second. I never shamed those I love. I just made it very clear that certain behaviors and outcomes were expected. Most of us rarely shame in an abusive manner, but when we define relationships through behaviors, shame is always involved. And when shame is involved, personal identity is always at stake. If you are a parent who is seeing the results you desire by using shame wrapped in "love," you may not see the problem. Shame can work for coercing positive behaviors, but it always does so at the expense of identity. When shame is the tool, identity is the currency. No matter how pleasant or kind a bishop is when he mentions to a youth group the importance of graduating from seminary or serving a mission, they will always interpret it as an identity challenge. *Just make sure you graduate from seminary and serve a mission, or else there is something wrong with who you are.* This isn't necessarily the bishop's fault, but it sure does tee up the adversary to attack through heart and identity. A behavioral influence can always be countered by an identity argument. If we fail to do the work of establishing a relationship of love and acceptance, the adversary has the upper hand every time. We will never win the battle of identity by playing in the arena of behaviors.

Of course, this identity battle extends to those we love; and part of our mission here on Earth is to be by their side, assisting them in overcoming the identity lies of the adversary. We naturally assume certain outcomes will place others on a path to realize their identity; in reality, desired outcomes will only give them more reason to misinterpret their personal identity. We act as if following a gospel equation focused on behaviors will bring people stability in life, and they may feel that they can start believing they are blessed children of God only when they achieve those behaviors.

In reality, it is the strength of our relationships that will pull them through this identity battle. When outcomes are diminished or even removed from these relationships, it does not decrease the likelihood of success or happiness—it increases people's ability to persist because they know they are accepted for who they are. This isn't to say we won't hope for positive, righteous outcomes to manifest at some point along their journey. Of course we will, but we have to recognize the adversary has a stronger counter-attack when we lead out with behaviors, and it involves shame every single time. Our goal should be to help reveal the true identity of those around us by offering our hearts, not by pushing behaviors. God already loves their eternal identity, and so when we offer our hearts and show them love, they begin to believe we love them as they are.

IS GOD DISAPPOINTED IN ME?

Another risk of using shame through behavioral-focused messaging is that it can alter the perceived purpose of Jesus Christ and repentance. When we push behaviors on people, and for whatever reason those people don't live up to those behaviors, they stop accepting their own identity, seeing themselves as broken or unacceptable. Everyone will make mistakes and sin, and if those we love don't accept themselves even in their shortcomings, they will assume *Christ* won't accept them either. Since the time of Adam, they have been hiding their negative behaviors from everyone around them and from God. They feel they have no choice but to hide the wounds that prove they are bad. The wounds fester as people bury them in shame and false identity, and this creates more trauma and hurt. Often, the "well-behaved boy" succumbs to the pressure of always trying to comply with the "good-boy" identity. His divine identity, which was loved and accepted from the beginning, gets buried deeper and deeper by the shame. This can sometimes lead to a rebellion that feels unexplainable. The boy who was once known as well-behaved and clean-cut becomes angry and seeks to reject any rule or principle because he's lost heart through years of obsessing on the behavior side of the continuum. Compliance to behaviors can ease the tension in certain relationships for a time. They attend seminary and go to church so that they avoid an argument at home. But we all find out that compliance doesn't always ease the tension in life. We learn that following the rules as a child keeps us out of trouble, but as an adult, following the rules doesn't always protect us from life's trouble or trauma. Unfortunately, our attempt to create well-behaved people communicates to them that we want perfect people who never really need a Savior—but that stymies their own opportunities for growth and grace.

KURT FRANCOM

Communicating Acceptance

In a culture of positive behaviors and outcomes, our children experience a near-constant prodding. *Be sure to go to seminary, don't forget to say your prayers, missions are awesome, temple marriage is the best kind of marriage, avoid pornography like the plague, etc.* There's nothing inherently wrong with these messages, but too many of these messages can drown out the message of personal identity and acceptance. One tactic we can employ to battle against the adversary's tool of shame through behaviors is to take time to regularly communicate full acceptance to those we love.

For example, one day I was riding in a car with my nephew who had just graduated from high school. It was just the two of us in the vehicle, so I was peppering him with questions about some of his future plans and ambitions. He was mission age, and it seemed apparent that a mission wasn't in his immediate plans. Seeing that I had his undivided attention, I could have reviewed with him the benefits and blessings of a mission and how much it positively affected my life. But I didn't think I had a strong enough relationship with him to lead out with behaviors; so instead I decided to communicate full acceptance. I said, "I know there is a lot of pressure for guys like you to serve a mission, but it doesn't matter to me. I think you're remarkably talented, and you will succeed in life regardless of the specific path you take. If you do ever have any questions about college or mission or anything, I'd be happy to talk about them." Much of what I said felt unnatural to me. There are few things I want more than to see my nephew grow from a mission experience, but he already knew that. But what I wasn't sure he knew was that I loved and accepted him, and so did his Savior.

On another day, a friend reached out to me on Facebook about his sibling who was in a same-sex relationship. He wanted to show

IS GOD DISAPPOINTED IN ME?

love to that sibling by attending their wedding even though he didn't agree with the premise of their marriage. He was also concerned that if he did attend the wedding, his sibling would share photos of the wedding on public social media sites, and since my friend was in a high-profile Church leadership position he wasn't sure how others would respond. I could see that he had a remarkable opportunity to communicate acceptance with his sibling. I encouraged him to attend the wedding and stand in photos, but not to wait until his sibling shared the photos. He should lead out and demonstrate his acceptance for his sibling by sharing the wedding photos on his own social media accounts. Some may judge, but his sibling will possibly feel his love and acceptance, and that is what matters most.

As I have shared that story with others, I have had some share the concern that attending a same-sex wedding may communicate that they condone or agree with same-sex marriage. That might be the case, but we cannot control how other people interpret our actions; we can only work toward communicating to those we love that we accept them. When we do that, our loved ones will be reinforced by the message that their Eternal Father loves and accepts them.

Another concern I often hear about showing acceptance is the fear that if our loved ones see us accepting them no matter what behaviors they make it can feel like we are actually encouraging them to go down paths not conducive with the covenant path. This is a valid concern. However, this is one of the great paradoxes we experience in mortality. Carl Rodgers explained it this way: "The curious paradox is that when I accept myself just as I am, then I can change."[60] Or another way to say this is, "The curious paradox is that when [my loved ones] accept [me] just as I am, then I can change." Again, love and acceptance provide the momentum-building force

167

on the Gospel Continuum. Receiving God's unconditional love builds the desire in us to swing toward righteous behaviors.

Modeling Grace

In our attempt to lead loved ones down a covenant path, whether as parents, Church leaders, or friends, we naturally want to perpetuate righteous habits in the lives of other individuals. This means we emphasize prayer, scripture study, programs like *Come Follow Me*, church attendance, showing respect and love for our prophets and other leaders, keeping the sabbath day holy, etc. All these efforts are intended to model what a gospel-living life is. Whether those we love fully embrace these religious habits or not, we know that when hard times come in life, they will always know how to pray. When tragedy strikes, they can recall comforting scriptures that they read in their Young Women class as a youth. Teaching these behaviors helps us model to those we love what the gospel looks like so they can implement the same behavioral strategy in their own life.

These habits listed above are important; however, they are only appendages to the core gospel of Jesus Christ, which is His atoning sacrifice. And what is at the core of His atoning sacrifice? G.R.A.C.E. So, out of all that we model and teach to our children and loved ones, is there anything more important than modeling grace? If grace is not modeled in our relationships with parents, siblings, and Church leaders, how will people ever recognize grace in their relationships with their Savior?

Sitting with this question has caused me to rethink how I personally approach parenting. My family may not pick up on the various habits I model for them. Maybe they won't understand how to study the scriptures or pray with all their hearts. But I hope my children will understand the infinite love and grace available to

IS GOD DISAPPOINTED IN ME?

them from their Savior, Jesus Christ. I hope they understand that there is never a reason to give up, no matter how many times they mess up. Redemption is always standing by.

I have realized that I am not only a parent to my children—I am their first example of what a parent looks like, and anything I say or do has the risk of being projected onto our Heavenly Father. I have to give myself a lot of grace personally because I know I will not live up to that standard. But the more I consider it, the more I want to try. I may not be able to give infinite grace like our Savior, but I can aim to give more than I gave yesterday. If I cause my children to identify according to behaviors, they might miss the relationship I want to have with them. And if they miss my relationship, they might miss God's relationship. If they have a dad who yells, they might assume they have a God who screams. If they have a dad who grounds them, they might assume they have a God who condemns. I want to lead out with love and acceptance and make behavioral management secondary. I want to define our relationship on grace so that we can approach behaviors together in a healthier way.

Recently my mother shared with me and my siblings a comic from the classic comic strip *Family Circus* by Bil Keane. It showed two children standing in front of an open refrigerator with their mother. The oldest child says to her mother, "Can you pretend you're Grandma just once and give us whatever we want?" Of course, this made me chuckle since this comic perfectly fits our family dynamic. My mother (a remarkable grandmother) is always packing her kitchen pantry with sugary snacks for my children's visits. I often joke with her that her pantry looks very different from how it looked when I was a child. After enjoying a good laugh with my parents and siblings, I began to ponder: Why is it that we tend to learn how to give grace more freely as we age? No matter how

169

good or bad my son acts when he visits Grandma's house, he always leaves with a bag of M&Ms. Grandma never reviews their behavior before giving them treats. When they visit Grandma's house, my children know she gives them love in the form of chocolate candies, fruit snacks, and hugs. Often as my child is standing in front of my mom's pantry, pointing at a delicious treat, my mother looks at me for a nod of permission to spoil them. I appreciate my mother respecting the boundaries we have as parents as we've determined how we will raise our children and how many unhealthy snacks they receive—she was once that mother too.

Now, I get it. Many parents reading this want to pat me on the head and say, *This is cute how you are talking about parenting as if we can just let them make their own decisions with no limits. Don't you know they will get drunk on sugar every day and never go to bed?* Of course, children need boundaries and limits, especially considering that their brains are still developing and, left to their own devices, they would most definitely make regrettable mistakes. I'm not promoting some radical laissez-faire form of leading. Boundaries and rules are crucial for the healthy development of a child, but when we assume our child will always act with malicious intent if we don't yank their chain with verbal warnings and lectures, we miss the pureness of their hearts. Those we love are not inherently evil; they are, in fact, inherently good. Again, if we are continually managing our loved ones' behaviors, they will only see our relationship as a series of behavioral transactions. They will grow up not fully understanding what grace is, and, most notably, they will not fully understand how grace *feels.* They will remember that they had to *do* certain behaviors to get certain rewards from Mom and Dad, so they must do certain behaviors to get anything from God.

IS GOD DISAPPOINTED IN ME?

As I have diligently attempted to move away from a behavior-focused relationship style and more toward a heart-filled, affirming style focusing on companionship, it's been more than difficult. Staying on the behavior side of the continuum is comfortable for parents because, as was mentioned before, shame works, and we often get the immediate outcomes we desire. When one of my children acted out of line, I was able to drag them toward the time-out chair to "teach them a lesson." Or if they weren't moving fast enough in their attempt to find their shoes before we headed out the door, I could raise my voice and threaten restrictions. But now, in my attempt to parent with heart, I'm required to slow down, sit with them, hear them out, and offer a hug of encouragement. Instead of causing more tears, I find myself with the opportunity to wipe them away. I feel my children trust me and are more connected to me.

To be perfectly honest, I still have *many* moments of behavior-focused parenting where I am irritable and tired and have to apologize later. Yet the progress that amazes me the most is not my children's progress; it's my own. I feel like I am on a sanctifying path. My children may not be *doing* the things I want all the time, but we are becoming something greater and more connected.

This heart-focused attempt at parenting isn't meant to turn our relationship from parent/child to buddy/buddy. No doubt, my children still understand who the parents are in the relationship, just as we understand who the God of this world is. At times I am not sure if I have an overactive child or if they have been possessed by some demon from the underworld. An outsider may observe our approach and wonder why we are letting our child *walk all over us* and may think we need to *take control of that child*, but I quietly remind myself I am working on our relationship, rather than on my child's conforming behaviors.

KURT FRANCOM

What About Sin and Boundaries?

We can feel safe sending our child out into the little-league soccer field knowing that there are rules, as well as game officials to enforce those rules, to keep our children relatively safe during the game. However, this mortal game called life is far from fair and safe. This is a fallen world, and the adversary is willing to go to any length to cheat, lie, and deceive to win more souls to his side. We can't dismiss a focus on behavior while little Jimmy smokes weed in his secluded basement bedroom. Children are not prepared to face the temptation in this world, which is precisely why they need us as parents. But we can focus on behavior hand in hand with love and acceptance.

A typical parent/child relationship that gets referenced regularly is the relationship between Alma the Younger and his son, Corianton. In Alma chapter 39, Alma speaks to Corianton and is concerned with the path that his son is on. This chapter can easily justify a behavior-focused parenting style. Alma appears to be in lecture mode and is giving it to his son, who has made some poor choices. In verse 7, Alma says, "And now, my son, I would to God that ye had not been guilty of so great a [behavior]. I would not dwell upon your [behaviors], to harrow up your soul, if it were not for your good." Having a grace- or heart-focused relationship does not mean that you are parenting wrong when you bring up or focus on behavior (especially when that behavior is sinful).

Often, "for [their] good," we as parents must address sinful behaviors and the consequences that follow. However, if we lead out with a focus on behaviors and make it the core focus of our parenting, it will only cause shame and damage the relationship we want with our children. Having an established relationship full of unconditional love and acceptance is crucial when it comes time to

IS GOD DISAPPOINTED IN ME?

address sin as a parent, especially when your child needs to address their sin with you. It would be foolish to expect that, as parents, we will create some bulletproof structure in our homes that will remove any chance that sin or mistakes will happen. When our children do sin, I pray we all have a stable relationship based on love and grace that will give them the strength to discuss their mistakes with us. Remember, children are not inherently evil, but that doesn't mean they will never sin. And when they do sin, and they are in desperate need of help to overcome that sin, what will they see in you? Will they see a loving coach ready to embrace them and help them figure out the next step? Or will they see you as focused solely on behaviors, ready to determine their punishments and further restrictions?

What If We Have It Backward?

This approach to relationships isn't as simple as flipping a switch. It requires time and practice, and, most importantly, it requires you as an individual to more fully understand your own divine identity. Stephen Covey once said this:

> You don't look at their behavior. You look at their divine identity and potential and treat them accordingly. How do you do that? Well, if you don't have deep within yourself this same sense, you can't. You may try to fake it, but it won't come genuinely, authentically, except the soul of those who sense it about themselves and their relationship to God, who gives us the eye of faith.[61]

Instead of punishment, offer to repair their heart. This is why the idea of a disappointed God can be so damaging to our own progress.

If we can't remove that disappointed God from our psyches, we will never be able to fully accept His grace; and if we can't accept His grace, we won't be able to give grace. Elder Neil L. Andersen put it this way:

> You can't become a grace-focused parent until you understand the grace God is offering you right now. The Lord has told us that if we come forward with a broken heart and a contrite spirit, He will not just repair our heart and cleanse our spirit: He will give us a new heart. "A new heart also will I give you, and a new spirit will I put within you: and I will take away the stony heart out of your flesh, and I will give you a heart of flesh. And I will put my spirit within you and cause you to walk in my statutes."[62]

It can feel like we have been given an overwhelming responsibility to influence others for good. From the moment we awkwardly support our child's floppy head the day they are born, we feel a deep desire to protect them from the world. Or we feel like we have been protecting our brother since the days of the schoolyard, and now we have to protect him from his own negative behaviors. It is overwhelming to try to influence those we love, especially when they seem so lost.

But what if we have it backward? What if they weren't given to us to develop? What if we were given to them so we could develop? What if the bedtime routine was more about teaching us patience than teaching them obedience? What if their pornography habit is more about teaching us to love them through a difficult time rather than teaching them to avoid evil? In the challenging moments of

IS GOD DISAPPOINTED IN ME?

relationships, I try to remind myself that it's not about my loved one being compliant to behaviors—not initially, at least; it's about me becoming more of a grace-filled support to them like my Father in Heaven is. It's about me learning more about righteousness, or the *right relationship.*

CHAPTER 11

Conclusion

In the summer of 2013, I was at home with my young daughter Devri while my wife was at work. Little Devri had just passed her first birthday and was getting so close to taking her first steps. On this day, as we relaxed in our family room, my daughter pulled herself up on her feet and began to take her first steps. I scrambled to pull my smartphone out of my pocket to start recording. I needed to capture this moment so that my wife could witness it as well. Little did I know, as I was capturing a fun developmental moment in my daughter's life, I was also capturing a deep lesson about the love God has for me and for all His children.

I am thankful today that I still have that recording saved. You see, as my little Devri took each step with a little uncertainty, she also showed budding confidence. As she realized she could walk, her excitement grew, and it became contagious. In the short video, you can hear my voice—an elated father excited to see his daughter progress. As I revisit this video even now, years later, I can see how my voice as an earthly father echoes the voice of an encouraging Eternal Father:

Me: Look at you walk! Oh, my goodness! I turn the
camera on, and you fall down!

KURT FRANCOM

Devri: *Laughing*

Me: Okay, let's do it again! Come on! Stand up! (I grab her hand and help her up on her feet.) Okay, here she goes!

(Devri continues to walk and laugh.)

Me: (Cheering her on) Yeah, it's so fun! Come this way now!

(As Devri tries to pivot, she falls to the ground.)

Me: Ohhhh, you can't pivot yet, huh?

(I offer her my hand.)

Me: Should we stand? Okay, here we go! Come on, Devri!

(She takes several more steps.)

Me: Oh, isn't that much easier than crawling?

(Devri falls again.)

Me: Ohhhh, you're going to fall down another bazillion times, but it will be worth it!

As I watch this video, it brings me to tears every time. I am so pleased in the progress of my daughter, and the love pours out of me. I was never disappointed when she tripped or fell. I didn't have time to be disappointed because, as her father, I was too concerned with trying to give her a hand to help her up and with the knowledge that she would soon walk. This video doesn't just bring me to tears because it is my daughter, but because I recognize my Heavenly Father's voice and tone in my voice. "Do we understand our Heavenly Father's anxiousness at our every effort to return to Him?

IS GOD DISAPPOINTED IN ME?

Even when we are still a great way off, He welcomes our return."[63] He is never disappointed in us! He is always cheering us on as we take our own mortal steps. Right when we think He is disappointed in us, we realize He is offering us a hand through our Savior, getting us back on our feet to try again. Before we know it, we are walking and then running and becoming more like Him in every way.

At the time of this writing, my other daughter Mariah is six months old. Have you ever had a six-month-old child look at you? They can't help but smile at you. It's a smile full of love. There is no hesitancy in their display of affection. They accept you one hundred percent and love you completely. It is another lesson we learn about the love of God through these small children. They look at you as God looks at you. You are loved, accepted, and not a disappointment.

In our quest to develop in mortality, it is pivotal that we accept the love He is offering us. This can seem like an abstract idea. How can one accept love? We can start accepting God's infinite love by releasing the shame and disappointment we feel about ourselves. We do that by halting any negative feelings we assume God is feeling about us.

When we release these negative feelings and the accompanying shame, we are then more prepared for personal development. When we completely embrace Godly acceptance and our full identity as God's beloved, we can then engage in mortality on a deeper level. In this state of mind, we see mortality as an arena in which God has placed us—not to define us, but to help us grow. He becomes our Eternal Coach as He works with us in the arena, and we have the potential to become like Him.

It is remarkable how God has taught me about His true, loving nature through my own experiences as a parent. One final experience

I'd like to share is a lesson I learned one day while I was out for a run with my five-year-old son, Taysom.

Taysom was sitting in the jogging stroller as we were running along a somewhat busy street. I was navigating around some obstacles on the side of the road, and for a moment Taysom thought the stroller might be out of control.

My son said, "Dad, are you there? Are you driving the stroller?"

I replied, "Yes, son, I'm right here."

With relief in his voice, he exclaimed, "Oh, I thought you were at home, and I was lost!"

Many of us may often feel the same way as we navigate life. We get caught up in the hectic, busy lives we lead, with obstacles around every corner. Like my son, we too might wonder if we are out of control or if God is pushing us anymore. We may feel He has become disappointed and has left us lost to find our own way home. However, it only takes a simple prayer to ask, "God, are you still there? Are you still pushing me?" You will discover He has never given up on you or abandoned you. He is pushing you. He loves you. He has never been disappointed in you.

Acknowledgments

Wow! Writing a book is hard. I began this journey way too long ago and hit many roadblocks on the path that I could not have overcome alone. I want to thank my wife for being a constant cheerleader from the sidelines, encouraging me to keep writing and editing. I want to thank some of my brothers from another mother—Steve Shields, James Willhite, Doug Nielson, and Chris Bennett. Many of the concepts I write about in this book I could not have understood without these brothers walking me on a journey of understanding God's love on a deeper level. My children Devri, Taysom, and Mariah influenced this book in so many ways by giving me experience as a father. Parenting has taught me way more than I expected.

A big thank-you to the many editors and beta readers who helped me think through this content and how to communicate it. It was a rough manuscript early on, and thanks go to people like Michele Preisendorf, Cassidy Wadsworth, Starla Butler, Allie Barnes, Garrett Kroon, Laney Hawes, Robert Mortensen, Geoff Openshaw, Arthur Boutin, Dave LeFevre, Kara Egbert, Adam Elsworth, Beau Sorensen, and Nathan Nelson. The staff at Eschler Editing was a godsend at just the moment I was humble enough to receive additional help.

I want to send a big thank-you out to so many people who are way smarter than I am but still encouraged me to share my thoughts with the world. John Hilton, from Brigham Young University, was one of those people who could have told me to stay out of the big leagues, but he continued to applaud me. Ganel-Lyn Condie was also an encouraging voice helping me navigate the publishing world. The Leading Saints newsletter audience deserves a bucket of gratitude as well, since they continue to find my writing thought-provoking and worth the pages of a book. I hope they all get a chance to read this book, and I hope it challenges their perspectives on God's love in a way that allows more of that love into their lives. Thank you to Dan Duckworth, Ross Richey, Michael Ramsey, Jessica Johnson, Lillian Angelovic, and the many other members of the board of directors and advisors at Leading Saints. This book is one piece in the greater mission of Leading Saints and, hopefully, will be followed by many more under the Leading Saints publishing name.

Of course, while writing this book, there were moments of clarity and understanding that could have only come through an Eternal Source. I recognize the incredible influence of the Holy Ghost. Granted, this book isn't scripture, but it was a sanctifying process to be a part of it as I felt an extra ability to articulate these concepts in a way I hope encourages those on the covenant path. May this book glorify God, Jesus Christ, and bring more of God's children into a right relationship with Him.

And thank you, reader, for picking up this book and giving God another chance to love you.

Notes

1. Ezra Taft Benson, "Jesus Christ—Gifts and Expectations," *BYU Speeches*, December 10, 1974, https://speeches.byu.edu/talks/ezra-taft-benson/jesus-christ-gifts-expectations/.

2. Jonathan Edwards, *The Works of President Edwards, ed. Sereno Dwight* (New York, NY: Burt Franklin, 1968), 458.

3. Edwards, 458.

4. Sarah Pierrepont Edwards, "Her Uncommon discoveries of the Divine Perfections and Glory; and of the Excellency of Christ by Sarah Pierrepont Edwards, 1710–1758," in *The Works of President Edwards: With a Memoir of His Life*, ed. Sereno Dwight, vol. I, (New York: G. & C. & H. Carvill, 1830), 171–190.

5. Benson, "Jesus Christ—Gifts and Expectations."

6. Russell M. Nelson, "Becoming True Millennials," Worldwide Devotional for Young Adults, January 10, 2016, https://www.churchofjesuschrist.org/broadcasts/article/worldwide-devotionals/2016/01/becoming-true-millennials?lang=eng.

7. *Oxford Languages*, s.v. "Disappointed, *adj.*," accessed July 18, 2023, https://www.google.com/search?q=define+disappointed&rlz=1C1CHBF_enUS894US895&oq=define+disappointed&aqs=chrome.69i57j0i512l2j0i15i22i30l7.3408j1j1&sourceid=chrome&ie=UTF-8.

8.	Quoted in John Bytheway, *When Times Are Tough: 5 Scriptures That Will Help You Get Through Almost Anything* (Salt Lake City: Deseret Book, 2009), 476, Kindle.

9.	Joseph Fielding Smith, *Teachings of the Prophet Joseph Smith* (Salt Lake City: Deseret Book, 1993), 121.

10.	Lynn G. Robbins, "Until Seventy Times Seven," *Ensign*, May 2018, 22.

11.	George Albert Smith, Conference Report, Oct. 1945, 117, quoted in *Teachings of Presidents of the Church: George Albert Smith* (Salt Lake City: The Church of Jesus Christ of Latter-day Saints, 2011), chap. 18, https://www.churchofjesuschrist.org/study/manual/teachings-george-albert-smith/chapter-18?lang=eng.

12.	C. S. Lewis, *Mere Christianity* (HarperCollins, 2009), 142.

13.	Dale G. Renlund, "Our Good Shepherd," *Ensign*, May 2017, 30.

14.	Brad Wilcox, Northstar Conference keynote speech, 2019, YouTube video, https://www.youtube.com/watch?v=dU-a94190JQ.

15.	Lucy Mack Smith, History, 1844–1845, book 7, page 6, josephsmithpapers.org.

16.	Spencer J. Condie, "A Might Change of Heart," *Ensign*, November 1993, https://www.churchofjesuschrist.org/study/general-conference/1993/10/a-mighty-change-of-heart?lang=eng.

17.	Ezra Taft Benson, *Teachings of Ezra Taft Benson* (Salt Lake City: Deseret Book, 1988), 79.

18.	Hans T. Boom, "Knowing, Loving, and Growing," *Ensign*, November 2019, 104; emphasis added.

19.	Jeffrey R. Holland, "Tomorrow the Lord Will Do Wonders among You," *Ensign*, May 2016, 124.

20.	"Relationships Before Progress: A Conversation with Tom Christofferson, President David Checketts and Bishop Bruce Larson," interview by Kurt Francom, *Leading Saints*, March 11, 2018, https://files.leadingsaints.org/wp-content/uploads/2021/04/14131521/Relationships-Before-

IS GOD DISAPPOINTED IN ME?

Progress-A-Conversation-with-Tom-Christofferson-President-David-Checketts-and-Bishop-Bruce-Larson-Transcript.pdf?_ga=2.91815065.2037037413.1689769748-601873080.1689769747.

21. Stephen R. Covey, *Six Events: The Restoration Model for Solving Life's Problems* (Salt Lake City: Deseret Book, 2004), 512, Kindle.

22. Covey, *Six Events*, 537.

23. Russell M. Nelson, "Choices for Eternity," Worldwide Devotional for Young Adults, May 15, 2022, https://www.churchofjesuschrist.org/study/broadcasts/worldwide-devotional-for-young-adults/2022/05/12nelson?lang=eng.

24. Covey, *Six Events*, 1296.

25. Russ Harris, *The Confidence Gap: A Guide to Overcoming Fear and Self-Doubt* (Massachusetts: Penguin Group Australia, 2011), 94, Kindle.

26. Brené Brown, *Dare to Lead: Brave Work. Tough Conversations. Whole Hearts* (New York: Penguin Random House, 2018), 78.

27. Barbara Smith, "A Conversation with Sister Barbara B. Smith, Relief Society General President," *Ensign*, March 1976, https://www.churchofjesuschrist.org/study/ensign/1976/03/a-conversation-with-sister-barbara-b-smith-relief-society-general-president.

28. Clint Pulver, "Be a Mr. Jensen," published in 2017, YouTube video, 3:12, https://www.youtube.com/watch?v=4p5286T_kn0.

29. Pulver, "Be a Mr. Jensen."

30. https://biblehub.com/greek/5083.htm.

31. *Heart of Man*, directed by Eric Esau (Sypher Studios, Mew Films, 2017), http://heartofmanmovie.com/.

32. Dallin H. Oaks, "Love and Law," *Ensign*, November 2009, 26.

33. Michael F. Bird, "Revisiting Riddles of Righteousness," Logos, https://www.logos.com/grow/hall-riddles-of-righteousness/.

34. Covey, *Six Events*, 900.

35. Neal A. Maxwell, "Repentance," *Ensign*, November 1991, https://www.churchofjesuschrist.org/study/general-conference/1991/10/repentance?lang=eng.

36. Covey, *Six Events*, 1293.

37. Neil L. Andersen, *The Divine Gift of Forgiveness* (Salt Lake City: Deseret Book, 2019), 1478, Kindle.

38. Brené Brown, "The Power of Vulnerability," recorded workshop, Sounds True, Inc., 2012.

39. I Am They, "Scars," *Trial & Triumph*, released 2018, https://www.azlyrics.com/lyrics/iamthey/scars.html.

40. John Eldredge, *Wild at Heart* (Nashville: Thomas Nelson, 2001), 1146, Kindle.

41. Philip Yancey, *The Jesus I Never Knew* (Grand Rapids: Zondervan, 1995), 2283, Kindle.

42. James R. Rasband, "Ensuring a Righteous Judgment," *Ensign*, May 2020, 13.

43. Donald L. Hilton, *He Restoreth My Soul* (San Antonio: Press Publishing, LLC, 2009), 5075, Kindle.

44. *The Chosen*, season 1, episode 1, "I Have Called You by Name," created by Dallas Jenkins, Out of Order Studios, 2019.

45. *The Chosen*, "I Have Called You by Name."

46. Andersen, *The Divine Gift of Forgiveness*, 269.

47. D. Todd Christofferson, "Abide in My Love," *Ensign*, November 2016, 48.

48. Russell M. Nelson, "Divine Love," *Ensign*, February 2003, 24.

49. Dieter F. Uchtdorf, "The Gift of Grace," *Ensign*, May 2015, 108.

50. Stephen Robinson, *Following Christ* (Salt Lake City: Deseret Book, 2004), 1891, Kindle.

51. Thomas S. Monson, "We Never Walk Alone," *Ensign*, November 2013, 124.

52. Russell M. Nelson, "Divine Love," *Ensign*, February 2003, 24.

53. Christofferson, *Ensign*, November 2016, 48.

54. Christofferson, *Ensign*, November 2016, 48.

55. Quoted in Joy D. Jones, "An Especially Noble Calling" *Ensign*, May 2020, 16.

56. Adam Miller, *Letters to a Young Mormon* (Provo: Neal A. Maxwell Institute for Religious Scholarship, 2014), 136, Kindle.

IS GOD DISAPPOINTED IN ME?

57. Miller, 110.

58. Covey, *Six Events*, 2659.

59. *Heart of Man*, http://heartofmanmovie.com/.

60. Carl Rogers, *On Becoming a Person: A Therapist's View of Psychotherapy* (New York: Houghton Mifflin, 1961), 466, Kindle.

61. Stephen Covey, *Six Events*, 795.

62. Andersen, *The Divine Gift of Forgiveness*, 2872.

63. Andersen, *The Divine Gift of Forgiveness*, 239.

Note to the Reader

Thank you for allowing me to share my perspective with you. I hope it has deepened your faith in some way. If you would like to help other people benefit from the contents of this book, please leave a positive review on Amazon. This will help those most needing to read this book to find it. If the messages in this book resonate with you, I invite you to visit LeadingSaints.org and subscribe to the *Leading Saints* podcast. You can also reach out to me with any questions or comments on that website as well.

About the Author

Kurt Francom is the founder and executive director of Leading Saints, a nonprofit organization dedicated to helping Latter-day Saints be better prepared to lead. He is also the host of the premier Latter-day Saint podcast *Leading Saints*, reaching five hundred thousand downloads per month, with a lifetime reach of twenty million total downloads as of 2023. Kurt graduated from the University of Utah in 2008 with a degree in business marketing. He ran a web-development company for five years before focusing on Leading Saints full-time in 2016. Kurt currently lives in American Fork, Utah, with his lovely wife, Alanna. They are blessed to have three children and a dog.